Reykjavik

Reykjavik

Gérard Lemarquis

INNERCITIES
Signal Books

First published in 2013 by
Signal Books Limited
36 Minster Road
Oxford OX4 1LY
www.signalbooks.co.uk

A catalogue record for this book is available from the British Library

ISBN 978-1-908493-82-8 Paper

Cover Design: Imprint Digital Ltd.
Production: Imprint Digital Ltd.
Cover Images: Pavel Svoboda/Shutterstock; Linda Hilberdink
Photography/Shutterstock
Maps: Sebastian Ballard
Printed in India

Contents

I would like to thank my wife Maria, my daughter Léa and James Ferguson of Signal Books.

Introduction

"What was your first impression when you landed here forty years ago?" It's something I am asked quite often, and it's true that first impressions are often the right ones, simple but accurate, while experience then complicates them with endless corrections and nuances. The Iceland I saw from the airplane on that first arrival was one of scattered white houses and green painted roofs. There are few green roofs left today, and what we think is permanent often proves to be ephemeral. The plane from Glasgow landed in the centre of Reykjavik, but for many years now international flights have landed at Keflavik. I was immediately struck by the air's icy clearness, by the way night had seemingly vanished but above all by the cold wind which, however much you expect it, cuts through you. I walked to the centre of town. On the way a drunk offered me some dried fish and a swig from his bottle of *brennivín*. A police car stopped and drove me to the campsite. It seems an improbable event now, when tourists arrive every day in the hundreds or even thousands.

Two-thirds of Iceland's population of about 320,000 live in Reykjavik and its suburbs. Yet in talking about this small city, the world's most northerly capital, you cannot help but talk about an entire country and an entire society that has perhaps changed more completely than any other European nation due to its rapid enrichment. Yet some things remain unchanged. Iceland is a country of fishermen forced for centuries to live from agriculture. It is an open society, always ready to seize what opportunities come its way. It committed terrible financial mistakes before 2008 but has been quick to start its recovery. It rejects—and has always rejected—foreign domination but is quick to absorb any number of outside influences, safe in the knowledge that it will always be protected by its island status and its remoteness. Its past and present have been formed by a small population in a large geographical area, battered by an inhospitable climate and natural disasters, but it has always found solutions to its problems and constraints.

Icelandic society is very self-absorbed. Like most insular societies it is constantly navel-gazing, constantly shifting between inferiority and superiority complexes, sometimes exhibiting both at the same time. Icelanders are susceptible to outside judgements, but only insofar as they confirm what they already think of themselves. They have always claimed a monopoly on their image, good and bad, and foreigners on short visits never tire of endorsing it. They invariably mention, for instance, that Icelanders are inveterate drinkers, whereas in fact they drink the least of any European people, and they do so because Icelanders have decided that this is *their* vice. This book tries to distinguish between the true and the false, the myth and the reality, not to repeat the old half-truths but to analyze and interpret. It has been written by a foreign observer who for three decades for Agence France Pressse and almost four for *Le Monde* has sought to decipher the Icelandic society of which he is part, but from an outsider's perspective.

This book is a journey through Reykjavik, a journey in space but also in time. It looks at what is most obviously visible—buildings and other landmarks—and also at what is less obvious in a small, intimate and sometimes secretive society. Two chapters focus on literature and the visual arts, but these can be nothing more than a survey, an invitation to read, look at and listen to what is available or, better still, to come to Reykjavik, a place that accords such importance to culture in all its forms.

There are some towns that when revisited after a period of time seem to have changed fundamentally, making the visitor feel that he or she recognizes little or nothing. Reykjavik is not one of them. The old town, those splendid wooden buildings clad in their corrugated iron, may have decayed in the 1960s and 1970s when concrete and demolition were the order of the day, but it survived and today is enjoying a second youth. Old Reykjavik slumbered in indifference but awoke, almost intact, when a new generation again recognized its beauty. Some things are gone forever. The stench of the fishmeal factory, what was called "the smell of money", no longer drifts over the city, as the processing plants have moved elsewhere. The trawlers, however, still come into the old port, the naval dockyard is still in the centre of town and the little fishing boats still tie up at the quayside in late afternoon during the summer.

But above all it is its extraordinary location that remains untouched: the volcanic Esja mountain range that shelters Reykjavik from the worst of the north wind, the bay littered with islands, the headlands which brave the storms. The setting is practically identical to that which witnessed the arrival of the first Vikings from Norway, and it will doubtless remain as such until a volcano or earthquake decides to rearrange it.

It is not only seismic shocks that have shaken Iceland, the collapse of the major banks in 2008 and the bankruptcy of an entire nation provoked an unprecedented social eruption. The proverbially calm and consensual Icelanders revolted to the point of near insurrection. Where in this part of the world had crowds gathered day after day to hurl abuse and missiles at parliament until the government fell? This was no spring, like in North Africa, but a revolt in the depths of winter, illuminated by the bonfires set up in front of the parliament building. I will return to this critical turning-point in Iceland's history, which for Reykjavikers constitutes a before and an after—financially, socially and culturally.

Thirty years ago, people said: "why bother to build hotels in Reykjavik? What tourists want is to see the country and nature." Nowadays many visitors come just for the capital, to walk in streets between sea and mountains, between storms and sunny spells, between sun, rain, sun and snow—and any other sort of weather. They come to feel both the warmth of the city's nights and the frozen beauty of its mornings.

Yet the first impression was still the right one. The clear air, the wind that cuts to the bone in any season, the white houses and the urban landscape that can be transformed by a single, scarce ray of sunshine. And then the taste of dried fish.

View from the tower of Hallgrímskirkja (Andreas Tille/Wikimedia Commons)

1 | Contours
Geography and Beginnings

This is a country of shifting light, intermittent brightness and darkness, of constantly changing weather. Far from the static splendour of a polar landscape frozen for eternity by cold and ice, here everything is green or black or white, but all elements are always extreme, even violent: the wind, the colours, the stark and precipitous contours of the natural world. Everything is movable, elusive, unpredictable, ultimately hard to grasp—nature of course, but also humans. Power, energy, rain, rust, clear nights, the smells of the sea—these ingredients make up Iceland and Reykjavik.

Whatever the weather, rain, snow or sun, dazzling or disconcerting, Iceland's light is spellbinding. As soon as a rare ray of sunshine licks the corrugated iron roofs of Reykjavik's old houses, walk to where you can catch sight of the sea, normally no further than the corner of the street because the water is omnipresent and visible from every point. Low light makes a sculpture of the landscape's rugged shapes, and even the briefest bright interval sets the snow-covered Esja mountain range ablaze. If in winter the mountain's snow stands out in sharp contrast to the dark sky, in summer it is green grass that struggles to climb the steep black slopes.

From the old port, which the fishing boats—unlike the containers ships—haven't yet deserted, there is a vista of sea and mountains. The weather is predictably changeable, veering between mild rain and cold brightness. Advertisements proliferate for puffin and whale-watching tours and off-road adventures in vast 4 × 4s, urging visitors to leave Reykjavik and explore the sea or the vast emptiness of the interior. But it is worth staying in the capital to discover its unique cultural life and its role in Iceland's turbulent history. Reykjavik is Iceland, its only metropolis and the centre of its political and social life.

Nature and Climate

With its 103,000 square kilometres, Iceland is the second biggest island in Europe after Great Britain (230,000 sq km). The island is much more southerly than its Scandinavian neighbours and does not deserve its Arctic reputation. Only the island of Grímsey falls within the Arctic Circle, and the country's northern coasts hardly extend further than 66° latitude. Disproportionately huge on world maps, Iceland is often missing on those of Europe or perhaps relegated into some unused corner—a cartographers' convention that is guaranteed to upset Icelanders.

Greenland, its nearest neighbour, is 287 kilometres distant. Iceland is closer to Scotland (789 km) than to Norway (970 km). And this is the primary Icelandic paradox: as a European country it is closer to North America; as a Nordic state it is nearer the United Kingdom than Scandinavia. All this is interpreted differently in an Icelandic primary school classroom. Here in geography lessons children learn that Iceland is no longer to the north of anywhere but rather in the centre—which is indeed where it is in strategic terms, the central link or hub within the North Atlantic.

Iceland has always been seen as a stopping-point on the way to somewhere else: for the Basques heading further north towards Jan Mayen; for the Vikings, who a millennium ago were attempting to reach the American continent. And today it is the obligatory port of call for tourist planes crossing from the Old World to the New, which have to stop to refuel.

Iceland's destiny is inseparable from that of the North Atlantic, where it acts as the most southerly gateway but as a gateway nonetheless. If the nerve centre of the world were to move towards Southeast Asia, Iceland's geographical location would become even less significant. Yet there is a remote hope: that one day shipping between Japan and Europe will take the shortest, albeit most difficult, route across the Arctic Ocean, in which case Iceland would witness a boost to its maritime importance.

Iceland can be read as an open book. Its landscape, like its language, has never been covered by the sediment of time. This landscape is an extraordinary lesson in geology, offering a catalogue of volcanic and glacial phenomena. The coastal plains, where almost the entire population lives, comprise no more than five or six per cent of the island's surface area. These are the areas that a tourist will drive through in a tour of the island. The mountains that he or she sees are in fact plateaux of differing layers and peaks which reach from 1,200 to 1,500 metres in the centre and south and between 800 and 100 metres to the east and west. In these latter areas they are carved apart by deep valleys that end in fjords. High mountain ranges covered with glaciers (*jökull*) dominate the centre of the country, the highest being Öræfajökull ("wasteland glacier") where Iceland's highest point, Hvannadalshnjúkur, stands at 2,119 metres. Snæfellsjökull, the starting-point for the heroes of Jules Verne's *A Journey to the Centre of the Earth* (1864), rises to 1,445 metres in the west of the island.

Iceland's emptiness fascinates visitors from overpopulated countries with its expanses of stone, ice, sand, lava, moss and lichen. Tourists like to fantasize about its empty spaces and these spaces willingly provide fertile ground for dreams, fears and all sorts of mysteries, as those who come from elsewhere find the vacuum so abhorrent that they need to fill it with the objects of their imagination. As for Icelanders, they more prosaically call the tundra and glaciers uninhabited space while farmers let their sheep graze on the edge of the emptiness. The 23 *sýslur*, Iceland's administrative divisions or counties, are only demarcated on three sides—the sea to the north or south and two vertical borders; in the uninhabited wilderness in the centre of the country they merge into one another.

It is impossible to judge distances; how far away, for example, is the snowdrift on the mountain in the distance: five, ten or fifty kilometres? No landmark in the foreground allows us to establish a sense of perspective, no tree in the background helps us guess at the scale involved. Visibility, a source of wonder in Iceland, is deceptive— and woe betide the rambler who casually sets off for a gentle climb at the foot of a glacier. The first crevasses are almost much further away than anyone imagines, for no desert worthy of the name does not have its own mirages. (The uninhabited expanses, to the regret of some, are now increasingly crisscrossed by 4x4 vehicles, which perhaps rob them of part of their mystery and in any case their inaccessibility.)

The low skies, black or grey, then the sudden gaps in the clouds when patches of sunlight sweep across the mountains, make the land an uncertain place. The wind seemingly follows no direction or changes constantly even blowing in different directions at once. You might be able to work out from where it is blowing but it is less easy to say what that direction is. In short, Iceland lives in a state of permanent draught and in a climate dominated by depressions.

Icelanders have a strange love-hate relationship with their climate, as if they have never quite got used to it from the earliest days of colonization. They tend to appreciate a grey, misty and windless day, but classify one that is sunny, dry, cold and windy as bad weather. Curiously, they view their weather—like their economy and culture—in a way more appropriate to a nation ten times bigger and situated in very different parts of the world. Icelandic sagas, masterpieces of medieval literature, almost never alluded to the weather, except on very rare occasions to record that a port was blocked by an ice-floe and that a sailing would thus be late. (Compare this with French or English medieval writing full of complaints against winter cold or the litany of laments in Italian literature at the slightest drop in temperature.) If good or bad weather is only defined by what the weather is like elsewhere or at another time of the year, Icelanders often seem to be simply affronted by the weather around them. They have, it is said locally, slept naked since the days of colonization, and that was well before geothermal technology transformed every home into a power station. It is often 25°C or more inside a Reykjavik home, partly because hot water is so cheap but also perhaps because excessive warmth is in the collective unconscious not only a right but a form of revenge.

There is no culture of coldness in Iceland, either in terms of architecture or clothing, and people in Reykjavik dress like people in London, Brussels or Berlin according only to fashion and irrespective of the weather. They have in recent years, however, rediscovered their traditional knitted wool, long rejected as entirely non-chic, and this may have something to do with tourists seeking out hats and sweaters made from *Lopi* wool which is marketed as rain-resistant.

Listening to the weather forecast is a true obsession, and if European television channels have generally transformed their forecasting into a sort of beauty contest nothing could be further from the truth in Iceland where the weather men and women are more reminiscent of preachers in some fundamentalist Protestant sect. Icelanders listen to the forecast at eight o'clock, at ten, at midday, in the afternoon and evening, and sometimes it can seem like something from a Beckett play with fine weather in the role of Godot. In short, people spend their time waiting for snow in winter and sun in summer.

It is easier to appreciate the general fixation with weather forecasts when we remember that Icelandic contains an infinite number of words and expressions to describe the weather; there are many terms applied to snow, wind and rain to evoke their consistency, texture and peculiarities. Like a soap opera with unexpected twists when anything may change from one moment to another, weather forecasts enjoy a huge following.

The tourists who come in summer are struck by the absence of night time and conclude that the country must descend into an endless darkness in winter. The truth is rather different as although sunrise and sunset are very close together both are preceded and followed by several hours of half-light (due to the obliqueness of the sun's rays) so that the actual amount of "daytime" is hard to count. Winter, in general, is mild in Reykjavik and long and harsh in the north. Temperatures fall rapidly in lower altitudes, but this hardly concerns the populated areas which are all situated on the coast. In the capital the temperature hovers at around zero, to the annoyance of plants which cannot decide whether to grow or die and children who can rarely skate two days running on Tjörnin, the small lake in the centre of town. Snow piles up on the mountains but rarely settles on the coasts except in the north, where the climate is more continental.

The Icelandic summer is cool, even cold at low altitudes where snowfall is not unknown. It is warmer and particularly sunnier in the north where there are fewer fjords. Spring, which comes late, and autumn, which arrives early, are hardly mentioned in Iceland, and the word *vetur* (winter) is used to designate the school year. This division of the year into two seasons has perhaps less to do with climate than culture; winter is a time for community events, theatre, music and social life, whereas summer has a centrifugal effect on people, scattering them apart—it is not the done thing to put on a show or arrange a meeting between 15 June and 15 September, as if everyone goes their own way only to meet up again at nightfall.

Contrary to popular belief, Iceland is not barren in flora and fauna. Several companies operating from Reykjavik's harbour offer boat excursions to watch whales and dolphins—and some 23 species have been recorded in Icelandic waters, the most common being the Minke whale. Visitors have to drive further afield to see seals sunbathing (when the sun shines) on the coastline at Ingólfshöfði peninsula.

Reykjavik and its surrounding countryside also boast a rich array of bird life. There are some species that are year-round residents, some who stay only for the summer and others who stop here to gather strength before setting off once more for Greenland. Migratory birds can be divided into short-haul species which migrate across the ocean to the British Isles or mainland Europe, and long-haul species, which fly all the way from Africa.

Spring, when breeding takes place, is the prime time for bird-watching, but so is autumn, when brent geese gorge themselves with food before heading off via Greenland to their breeding grounds in Canada. Whooper swans, meanwhile, breed in the summer in Iceland and then fly up to two thousand kilometres south to overwinter in southern England. The two emblematic birds of Iceland are the ptarmigan and the puffin, the former—brown in summer and white in winter—forming a favourite Icelandic meal on 24 December. Ptarmigans can be seen a few kilometres outside Reykjavik, while the main populations of puffins are to be found in the Westman Islands (although some can be spotted on whale watching expeditions from Reykjavik). These, too, are eaten, though the tourist authorities try not to discourage the sentimental affection that surrounds these likable birds.

Each terrain has its own flora, and in the warmer months many types of flowers follow one another, with those dandelions and buttercups that escape the lawnmower forming huge yellow carpets. The lava fields are the habitat of mosses, lichens and various types of berry. Visitors at the beginning of August will find a profusion of blueberries, small but delicious. In September the lava field flora is most spectacular with the hues of autumn, and those who venture onto the slopes of Esja close to Reykjavik will be surprised to find at a height of a few hundred metres the sort of vegetation that is normally to be seen at over three thousand metres in the Alps. Flora is admittedly rare and struggles to survive, such as saxifrages when the snow melts or moss campion in the summer, but walkers may come across an angelica close to a stream, a giant at over two metres that seems to defy the climate and whose seeds are believed to hold curative properties. In June the lupin flowers, creating valuable humus in the most arid areas with its nitrogen-rich roots. Trees can be planted where lupins have colonized and enriched the soil, but the flower is often rampant and can be over-invasive.

Myth of Founding

The Norwegian Ingólfur Arnarson set sail for Iceland with his blood-brother Hjörleifur in the second half of the ninth century. After a great deal of rape and pillage en route they finally reached the island where their greed was excited by the sight of great areas of virgin land. They were not the first to have travelled this way, but few Vikings had risked the sea routes before them.

Having taken on supplies of slaves in Ireland, Ingólfur and Hjörleifur landed on Iceland's south coast in two separate ships in 874 (or so it is still taught). Hjörleifur, who established a settlement on the promontory that still carries his name, was quickly killed by his Celtic slaves, known as the "men of the west", who fled to what were baptized the Westman Islands. Ingólfur had meanwhile sailed towards another promontory, today Ingólfshöfði, where he had his ceremonial sculpted high seat pillars (or chair backs) thrown overboard, announcing that he would build his settlement where they landed ashore. The two slaves sent to look for them eventually found them in the small bay of what is now Reykjavik. The pillars had fortuitously come ashore at the place on the island where the climate is most clement. A painting, signed P. Raadsig and dated 1850, shows Ingólfur ordering the men to erect the pillars while he and a group of men, women and children look on.

The term *saga* in Icelandic refers to history with a capital H, as well as to stories . . . As such the sagas have been a rich source of confusion and contradiction, not least the story of Ingólfur, as told in *Landnámabók* or the "Book of Settlement". In the periods of nationalism preceding and following independence in 1944, the sagas were often taken as literal truth, but archaeological discoveries have questioned their veracity. It was already known that Irish monks had previously come to Iceland, but nowadays there are grounds to believe that Vikings had settled here as much as two centuries earlier. Nonetheless, the statue of Ingólfur Arnarson, standing between the headquarters of government and those of the Central Bank in Reykjavik, continues to vouch for the historical existence of the man it is meant to represent even if the museum supposed to bring his home to life has given up Viking myth-making and is modestly called 871 +/-2 to convey uncertainty about precise dates.

The myth of origin revolves around a hero whose parentage remains unknown: Ingólfur is considered an Icelander (the Embassy of Iceland has protested on several occasions to the relevant authorities when he has been honoured as a Norwegian abroad). But he must remain an enigma, with only those floating high seat pillars indicating his final destination like Moses' basket. Like the Nordic version of Romulus and Remus, the sworn brothers Ingólfur and Hjörleifur founded Reykjavik, and appropriately one of them was destined to die. The founding act consisted of the extermination of an ethnically different group.

Reykjavik and Around

Reykjavik is surrounded by sea to the north and south but benefits from many forms of protection. To the west is the cape of Kópavogur then the Álftanes peninsula (where the President of the

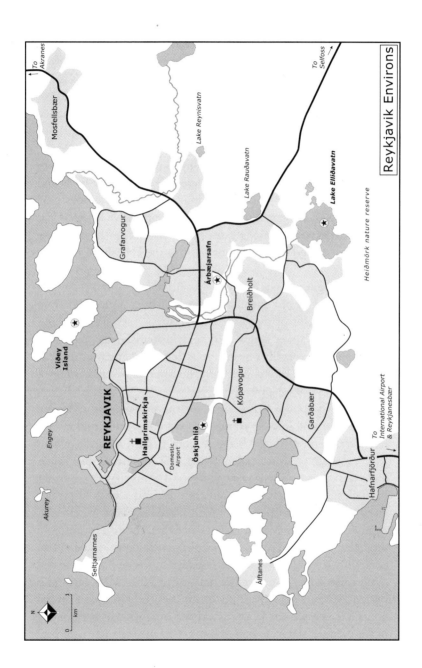

Reykjavik Environs

Republic of Iceland's residence stands), protecting the capital from high tides. The road leading to the presidential residence is open and nothing stops the curious visitor from approaching, but this is not the done thing, just as when a celebrity wanders about the centre of town people pretend not to notice. Reykjavik society is miniscule and it has tacit rules so as to avoid the security barriers and privacy issues of bigger cities.

To the south, the Reykjanes peninsula protects Reykjavik from strong winds. The last settlements here give way to lava fields and clumps of blueberry bushes before bizarrely shaped volcanoes, running from east to west, form a solid and impregnable barrier. Here people ski in winter among geysers and columns of rising steam. This steam emerges from the boreholes of the Hellisheiði geothermal power station, the second biggest of its sort in the world and a major supplier of electricity for local industries. The protective screen offered by the mountains can be better appreciated from the vantage-point of the international airport beyond the range. Here the wind never seems to drop, and tourists emerging from the airport are generally shocked by both the howling wind and the temperature. They should not worry, however, as Keflavik is one of Iceland's most inhospitable spots.

The airport was at first built for the purposes of a US-run NATO base, and initially travellers had to pass through the military base in order to reach the civilian airport, an arrangement which was not to all Icelanders' liking. The Americans then subsidized the construction of a new, connected terminal with a corridor through the base. Left-wing opinion in Iceland, always suspicious of American motives, was opposed to building what it perceived as an excessively large facility, but since then the airport has been expanded twice as growing intercontinental traffic and tourism as well as Icelanders' liking for holidays in the sun have boosted airport use. Long gone are the days when Icelandair's customers waited for hours in badly heated sheds for planes that were several hours late because the fleet was old and unreliable or because fog in Luxemburg, the main hub in Europe for the Icelandic company, was preventing landings. In the 1960s and 1970s travellers had to wait patiently among soldiers on leave while drinking their first beer. Beer was banned in Iceland until 1986, but not at the international airport. Nowadays it is allowed and available in Iceland, but locals, especially those of a certain age, have never got out of the habit of drinking beer on an empty stomach, even at seven in the morning, before getting into a plane. The airport, like all buildings designed by foreigners in Iceland, makes ample use of local materials, especially the mineral liparite, which most Icelanders seem never to have discovered.

The road linking Keflavik to Reykjavik was the country's first all-weather highway, and although most roads in Iceland are now paved even the main circular route was an unmade track forty years ago. The road to Keflavik was bad and traffic so sparse that protestors against the American presence could walk along it once a year, their backs turned towards the enemy as they headed towards Reykjavik. Today the NATO base is closed, the US military having left Iceland at short notice in 2006 despite a concession allowing them a lease of 99 years. The Keflavik road has since been turned into a motorway and until 2008 was bathed in generous lighting thanks to the country's supply of cheap geothermal electricity (since the economic crisis every other lamppost has been switched off).

Esja and Akranes

The imposing Esja range shelters Reykjavik from the north wind and reaches its highest point at just over 800 metres. The climb to its peak is one of the most popular outings for Reykjavik's inhabitants as it is relatively easy and leads to sweeping views of the Reykjanes peninsula. It was believed at the beginning of the twentieth century that there was a seam of gold at its summit and prospectors created the track that walkers still follow today. The first sheep to be seen outside the capital appear on Esja, fearlessly climbing up the steep slopes where grass gives way to rock, minerals and basalt eroded by rain, wind and snow.

Akranes, the first settlement to the north of the capital, can be seen from Reykjavik whatever the weather. Until recently it was reached by ferry as otherwise travellers had to take the long road around Hvalfjörður ("whale-fjord"), which owes its name to a legend rather than (as is popularly believed) to a whaling station where finback whales are cut up before being sent to Japan (Icelanders prefer the minke whale for its more delicate meat which in any case they eat sparingly). Nowadays a tunnel allows motorists to avoid the road around the shores of Hvalfjörður and take a short cut, but any visitor keen on spectacular landscapes may prefer to avoid the tunnel. As a result Akranes has become a distant suburb of Reykjavik, and although jobs have been lost in cement production and fishing, two big metal-processing factories have boosted employment.

Visibility, as has already been mentioned, is a unique phenomenon in Iceland as lack of pollution and clear skies due to wind allow one to see as far as a hundred kilometres away—and clearly. (This is far removed from the experience of the English and French who can just about make out each other across the Channel.) Looking north from Reykjavik we can first make out Akranes on its promontory. Beyond stand out the mountains of the Snæfellsnes peninsula with its extinct volcano to the west, which when not entirely covered in snow in mid-summer looks something like Mount Fuji. This volcano, Snæfellsjökull, is in fact a glacier and it is here that Jules Verne has his expedition descend into the earth and follow underground paths and caverns until they emerge through an erupting Mount Stromboli.

Still facing northwards, beyond the islands scattered throughout the bay, we again see Esja. To the east one passes around it to reach whale-fjord, but to the west one moves inland passing the home of Halldór Kiljan Laxness, Nobel literature laureate in 1955, which has now become a museum. The transition from city into nature is abrupt, and soon we are in a flat and sometimes monotonous region of water and low skies. Yet, suddenly and unexpectedly, appears a revelation: a vast lake with an island in its middle and a tortured landscape of rifts and fissures. Here is where the tectonic plates of Europe and North America are gradually separating in the process known as continental drift. The lake and rock formations are parts of a protected area under the aegis of UNESCO, and the Þingvellir National Park also has significance as the site of the *Althing*, the celebrated tenth-century open-air parliament (see Chapters 3 and 12). If Reykjavik is better protected from the elements, Þingvellir is more accessible from any part of the island—by horse, of course—and this may explain why it was chosen for the old parliament. Nowadays visitors can camp, fish, walk, immerse themselves in Iceland's history or, once a year in autumn, pick blueberries.

Returning from Þingvellir, we are likely to come across one or more of Reykjavk's suburbs—Mosfellsbær, Grafarholt, Grafarvogur—where signs of the recent economic crisis are clear: a shopping centre that never opened, half-built homes and offices, others hardly started. The cranes were taken down after the banking crash of 2008 but concrete carcasses lie around waiting for building to start again. Both the crisis and the rise in petrol prices have made it less attractive to live in the new suburbs where a lack of trees emphasizes poor architectural standards. Conversely, traffic has reduced in density since 2008 and, as a result, the morning and evening traffic jams.

Getting out of Reykjavik southwards involves a climb to reach the desert-like Hellisheiði plateau where uncovered chalk gravel alternates with lava fields and lichen. The Red Lake (Rauðavatn) is so-called because of its iron deposits and it gives off a pinkish reflection at certain times of day, the best being sunset when Iceland's charm, far from the suburbs, lies most clearly in its unspoiled nature. In mid-wilderness, however, is a small petrol station whose owner is a local radio celebrity. When the road is impassable drivers turn round and seek refuge over a coffee in his shelter, perhaps listening to his cheerful radio commentary.

Further on to the right the Hellisheiði geothermal power station offers a novel and exciting visitor experience. The plumes of steam escaping from the installation can be seen from afar and may evoke traditional images of hell, but inside the comfort is entirely Scandinavian. While in the main hall high-tech machinery performs the alchemy of turning hot water into electricity, workers behind glass screens watch over control panels and move silently around in their slippers. The Hellisheiði plateau, outside the power station, is no place to admire the landscape, as more often than not it is shrouded in cloud. But descent brings a break in the clouds and there are views again, especially of Hveragerði, whose greenhouses provide the capital with tomatoes, cucumbers and cut flowers. People come here to recover from illness or perhaps to return to the straight and narrow after an alcoholic detox, one of the favourite local pastimes. From here the traveller can press on to Selfoss and make any necessary purchases for a trip further south; there are a few food stores over the next 500 kilometres but nothing much else, and settlements by the road around the island are infrequent.

Rich in Resources

"We're rich because there are few of us in a huge land," declared recently the former business minister Gylfi Magnússon. And, he added, "It's because of this wealth that we've allowed ourselves to run our country so badly."

There is certainly a good deal of space in Iceland. The interior of the country is uninhabited. The coastline and rivers are under private ownership, access to beaches is free, but driftwood (from Siberia) belongs to the owner of the coastal land. In this country of strong social-democratic traditions, the right to land ownership is paradoxically more jealously protected than in the United States. Fishing rights in salmon rivers are sold at astronomical prices by those who own the land crossed by the rivers. The wealthiest rent private access to certain rivers.

The third and final "Cod War" between Iceland and Britain ended in the summer of 1976 with a British withdrawal from Icelandic waters. As trawlers from Hull and Grimsby clashed— luckily with no loss of life—against Icelandic coastguard vessels that cut their nets with giant scissors, Prince Charles was coming each year to spend a few days in Iceland fishing for salmon in a river in the east of the country. When the fame of the singer Björk was at its peak the country's conservative Prime Minister Davíð Oddsson wanted to grant her exclusive use of an island in the Breiðafjörður bay complete with abandoned lighthouse. The plan came to nothing.

On 9 January 2012 an unusual advertisement appeared in the local press:

> Svefneyjar Islands in Breiðafjörður bay. Habitable, price negotiable. Approximately 60 islands, the biggest slightly smaller than Flatey [the best-known in Breiðafjörður], 1.5km by 0.5km, 2 restored houses, one 229m², 10 rooms, the other 100m², 5 rooms, stables, sheep-fold, 2 barns, trout farming equipment, shed for agricultural vehicles, covered speedboat included. Landing possible on meadow. Eider ducks nesting, potential for commercial exploitation of seaweed and lumpfish.

Another proposed business deal had caused scandal in Iceland for several months in 2011 when the interior minister Ögmundur Jónasson of the radical Left-Green Movement announced his opposition to the planned sale of 30,000 hectares of land to a Chinese national. Iceland is three times the size of Belgium, has a density of three people per square kilometre and the land in question, called Grímsstaðir on the Mountain, is hardly an attractive proposition. The circular Route 1 passes through it in the north-east of the island, but it is sixty kilometres from the sea, high, windswept and the holder of the unenviable record for the lowest temperature ever recorded in Iceland. Only wild geese tend to stop there.

The would-be buyer, Huang Nubo, was proposing to build a 250-room hotel in this unlikely spot, and in the autumn of 2011 he promised much more while on a visit to Iceland: a health and fitness centre next to the planned hotel, family accommodation, a golf course and not least a five-star 300-room luxury hotel next to the brand new Harpa concert hall in Reykjavik. The Húsavik council fathers, close to the property for sale, seized their calculators and worked out that the providential buyer was going to invest the equivalent of €163 million, enough to boost employment for the foreseeable future.

Born in 1956, Huang Nubo is the president of the Beijing company Zhongkun Investment Group, with interests in the US and Scandinavia. Before going into business he worked for the Chinese

Communist Party in the field of propaganda and is still vice-president of a state-owned publishing organization. *Forbes* magazine estimates that he is the 125th wealthiest individual in China. When his many responsibilities allow, he is a keen climber and a poet, executive director of the Chinese poetry association. Icelandic poets invited to China came back enchanted.

Such glowing qualifications failed, however, to impress Reykjavik's diplomatic community, who saw the proposed land purchase as a first foothold for the day when—climate change permitting—the shipping route to the north of Siberia would be free of ice and open and Iceland would be a staging post on that route. Some even suspected that this huge and inaccessible area would one day serve as a dry dock for international shipping. Why else, they argued, build a hotel in the snow and a golf course on land that is frozen most of the year?

The project, which was still-born, recalls another, earlier foreign scheme. In the 1860s the French, who had a large fishing fleet, asked permission to build a base in a fjord on the west of the island, Dýrafjörður, for producing salt cod. The Danes, at that point masters of Iceland and loyal allies of France, had no objection to the plan, but the British were suspicious and applied pressure on Denmark—the question of sea routes and maritime advantage was already on the agenda. It is interesting to consider that if the French fishing base had been built it would have had a bigger population than the tiny Reykjavik of the time.

Global Hub

Strategic importance comes and goes, and some places in the world will always be significant as links or stepping stones between countries or continents. But Iceland is an anomaly; to the north there is nothing; westwards there is Greenland, barely 300 kilometres distant but almost unknown as far as the two peoples are concerned; to the east lies Russia and the potential of the Siberian sea routes. Before the advent of the airplane Iceland's geostrategic value was minimal. Much earlier, however, the Vikings had been masters of the sea, their navigational techniques highly advanced and in their time Iceland was something of a global hub. It was from here that the Vikings left for Greenland, then reached the shores that today belong to Canada.

There were many expeditions to Greenland, related in *Landnámabók*. Settlements have been unearthed there and it is estimated that the population may have numbered as many as 3,000. These people formed an independent community and like the Icelanders enjoyed a constitution and a similar set of laws. This much has been established, but what is still a matter for debate is the decline of that population until its eventual disappearance. Were the settlers massacred by indigenous people, or did they become extinct by failing to reproduce? They no longer had links with Iceland, they were entirely isolated and the decline in their livestock, according to archaeologists, parallels that of the settlers themselves. The rest is pure conjecture.

The adventures of the legendary Eric the Red began with a founding crime—like those, we have seen, of the "founder" Ingólfur Arnarson. He was outlawed and banished after killing Eyjólfur Saur (the Foul) and Hrafn (the Dueller):

He put out to sea past Snæfells Glacier. He found the country he was seeking and made land near the glacier he named Mid Glacier; it is now known as Bláserkur. From there he sailed south down the coast to find out if the country was habitable there. He spent the first winter on Eirik's Island, which lies near the middle of the eastern settlement. In the spring he went to Eiriksfjord, where he decided to make his home. That summer he explored the wilderness to the west and gave names to many landmarks there. He spent the second winter on Eiriks Holms, off Hvarfs Peak. The third summer he sailed all the way north to Snæfell and into Hrafnsfjord. Then he turned back and spent the third winter on Eiriks Island, off the mouth of Eriksfjord.

He sailed back to Iceland the following summer and put in at Breidafjörður. He named the country he had discovered Greenland, for he said that people would be much more tempted to go there if it had an attractive name. Eirik spent the winter in Iceland. Next summer he set off to colonize Greenland, and he made his home in Brattahlíð in Eriksfjord.

It is said by learned men that in the summer in which Eirik the Red set off to colonize Greenland, 25 ships sailed from Breidafjord and Borgarfjord, but only fourteen reached there; some were driven back, and some were lost at sea. (Translation Magnússon and Pálsson)

The thorny question of whether Leif Ericson, Eric the Red's son, explored what is known as Vinland (Newfoundland in modern-day Canada) also revolves around inconsistent and unreliable evidence. There are two categories of "proof": the sagas of the discovery of America on the one hand, and the archaeological research on the other. The sagas, written two or three centuries after the events in question (c.999 AD), cannot be considered a reliable source. In the case of the Vinland expedition, moreover, they are contradictory, as Jónas Kristjánsson, the great Icelandic specialist in medieval manuscripts, has demonstrated. As for archaeological findings, a single settlement called L'Anse aux Meadows suggests a link with Leif Ericson. The Vikings probably followed the coast of present-day Canada southwards, but nobody knows how far, and the vines mentioned in the sagas should not overheat imaginations as there are wild vines in Canada that can stand the cold.

On the 500th anniversary of Christopher Columbus' "discovery" of America some bold hypotheses were advanced in Iceland. The most adventurous theorists, like Ólafur Egilsson, maintained that Columbus had been in Iceland some years before his expedition and had learnt there of the transatlantic route. Others, wishing to give Icelandic explorers the credit for discovering America, imagined the following scenario: Basque ships came to hunt whales near Iceland's coasts up to the sixteenth century and in the process their crews heard of Icelandic discoveries in the American continent. Discussing these adventures over a drink in the taverns of Lisbon (not far from the Basque Country), they mentioned the exploits of

Eric the Red and Lucky Leif. As he sat nearby, pondering his failure to gain support at the Portuguese court, Columbus overheard these conversations—and the rest, of course, is history.

"Wicked" Freydís

Icelandic feminists recently complained about the small role accorded to women in the country's official history. Freydís, sister of Leif and daughter of Eric the Red, is a conspicuous exception, and the *Grænlendinga Saga* (Saga of the Greenlanders) depicts a woman of exceptional character and ambition who lived in Greenland and wished to get to Vinland as she knew that the transatlantic expeditions "were considered a good source of fame and fortune". She asked her brother Leif to give her the homes he had had built in Vinland, but he refused, saying he would rent them to her but not hand them over as a gift. She thus went to find two brothers with whom to launch an expedition that was to consist of two boatloads of thirty men (not including women) who were in a fit state to work. But Freydís cheated and put five more men in her boat than in the other, and when they landed she refused to let the brothers make use of Leif's houses, which they accepted, building others further away and saying, "We brothers could never be a match for you in wickedness."

The two settlements tried to coexist, playing games together, but tension soon mounted and the games and contact between them stopped. Envy and ambition were gnawing at Freydís who more than anything wanted to seize the two brothers' boat and who devised the following scheme:

Early in the morning Freydís got up and dressed, but did not put on her shoes. There was heavy dew outside. She put on her husband's cloak and then walked to the door of the brothers' house. Someone had just gone outside, leaving the door ajar. She opened it and stood in the doorway for a while without a word. Finnbogi [one of the brothers] was lying in the bed farthest from the doorway; he was awake, and now he said, "what do you want here, Freydís?"

"I want you to get up and come outside with me," she replied. "I want to talk with you."

He did so, and they walked over to a tree-trunk that lay beside the wall of the house, and sat down on it.

"How are you getting on?" she asked.

"I like this good country," he replied. "But I dislike the ill-feeling that has arisen between us, for I can see no reason for it."

"You are right," she said, "and I feel the same about it as you do. But the reason I came to see you is that I want to exchange ships with you and your brother, for your ship is larger than mine and I want to go away from here."

"I shall agree to that," he said, "if that will make you happy."

With that they parted. Finnbogi went back to his bed and Freydís walked home. When she climbed into bed her feet were cold and her husband Thorvard woke up and asked why she was so cold and wet. She answered with great indignation. "I went over to see the brothers to offer to buy their ship, because I want a larger one; and this made them so angry that they struck me and handled me very roughly. But you, you wretch, would never avenge either my humiliation or your own. I realize now how far I am from my home in Greenland! And unless you avenge this, I am going to divorce you."

He could bear her taunts no longer and told his men to get up at once and take their weapons. They did so, and went straight to the brothers' house; they broke in while all the men were asleep, seized them and tied them up, and dragged them outside one by one. Freydís had each of them put to death as soon as they came out.

All the men were killed in this way, and soon only the women were left; but no one was willing to kill them. Freydís said, "give me an axe."

This was done, and she herself killed the women, all five of them. After this monstrous deed they went back to their house, and it was obvious that Freydís thought she had been very clever about it. She said to her companions, "if we ever manage to get back to Greenland I shall have anyone killed who breathes a word about what has just happened. Our story will be that these people stayed on here when we left."

Early in the spring they prepared the ship that had belonged to the brothers and loaded it with all the produce they could get and the ship could carry. Then they put to sea. They had a good voyage and reached Eriksfjord early in the summer. (*Graenlendinga Saga*, translation Magnússon and Pálsson)

Freydís was clearly a strong woman, and unusually for the sagas of the period, it is she who has the leading role with her husband a mere accessory. It is also worth noting that matrimonial law was remarkably egalitarian, and by threatening to divorce her husband she was also threatening to leave with half of their shared wealth. The text is surprising in its modernity, and there is little sentimentality or affectation in the sagas with characters expressing themselves with extraordinary economy. Freydís, a Nordic Valkyrie who thinks nothing of sailing between Greenland and the coast of North America, is evocative of the cinematic *femmes fatales* of the 1940s, a prototype Bette Davis or Joan Crawford. If many women of the period behaved like her the archaeologists need look no further for the reasons that the Viking settlements simply disappeared.

Taken Prisoner

The only boats to risk the seas around Iceland at the end of the Middle Ages were those of Basque fishermen in pursuit of whales, prized not for their meat like today's Japanese gourmets but for whale-oil for lighting homes. The Basques did not, however, set foot on Iceland itself as any crew that was shipwrecked there would be promptly massacred. Only the English and Scandinavians risked visiting Iceland during its centuries of isolation. There was one notable exception, the so-called *Tyrkjaránið* or Turkish abductions of 1627, an episode that even now seems shrouded in mystery. The most common version of events relates that Turkish aggressors from Algiers (then under Ottoman rule) raided the Westman Islands and seized scores of Icelanders to be sold as slaves in North

Africa. Denmark, then in control of Iceland, was forced to pay an onerous ransom and some of the prisoners were eventually allowed to return to Iceland. The most famous of these captives, Guðríður Símonardóttir, married the pastor and poet Hallgrímur Pétursson, to whom the biggest church in Iceland, Reykjavik's Hallgrímskirkja, is dedicated.

The author Úlfar Þormóðsson has written novels based on the travels of these Icelanders and has looked into the experiences of Christian slaves on the Barbary Coast. When the Jews, Moors and anybody else considered by Spain to be infidels or renegades were expelled, they settled in large numbers in the Low Countries and in North Africa, particularly in Rabat and Salé in Morocco. European Protestants were at that time allies of Muslims against the Catholic countries of southern Europe. The Danes then had significant economic interests in North Africa, particularly in port administration and the collection of duties. While a Catholic country like France was opposed to the exchange of prisoners, believing that nobody was better as a galley slave than a Turk, the Ottomans themselves were open to the idea of ransoming slaves. The operation known as the Turkish abductions, it has been established, was in part led from Holland, a Protestant country and a supplier of arms to the Barbary Coast, and by renegades or Christian converts. Whether or not they received assistance within Iceland itself is another, as yet unanswered, question.

Changing Planes

From the beginning of the nineteenth century Iceland began to receive individual visitors, but the country had to wait until the twentieth to play a significant geostrategic role when the NATO base tracked the movements of Soviet submarines. The collapse of the USSR put paid to Iceland's military importance, but tourism has since filled the gap left by the departing Americans.

The airport at Keflavik remains an international hub, modest but nevertheless an important place for connecting flights. An American coming to Europe has every incentive to travel with Icelandair since although there are cheaper options for flying simply to Iceland, if the visitor books two flights with a connection at Reykjavik, the price drops dramatically despite the heavy airport taxes that were hitherto subsidized by the Americans.

In the 1970s the International Air Transport Association was attempting to establish a single price for all transatlantic flights, but the Icelandic company managed to avoid such regulation and undercut competitors by creating the fiction of two separate and independent companies whereby passengers would disembark from one airline at Keflavik and board another—both owned by Icelandair. Deregulation ended this one-stop subterfuge but since the financial crash and collapse of the Icelandic *króna* tourism has been in rude health. The industry has been growing rapidly, too rapidly perhaps for tour companies that promise their customers immersion in unspoilt nature, but travellers using the country as a stopping-point between the US and Europe remain in the majority.

Nature Reshaped

Reykjavik itself is at little risk of volcanic eruption, not being situated above a volatile mantle plume or volcanic "hot spot", but the capital is close to the fault line, which runs through the Þingvellir National Park, where the tectonic plates of Europe and North America are slowly separating by about two centimetres each year. The earth's crust finds its equilibrium at the cost of intermittent earthquakes that can affect Reykjavik—an earthquake in May 2008 caused some damage and injuries in nearby Selfoss—but building regulations are so stringent that a major disaster is unlikely. The nearest active volcanoes are at least a hundred kilometres away from the capital. Eyjafjallajökull, notorious for its disruptive ash clouds, occasionally covers gardens and cars with a thin film of dust.

But geothermal instability has its advantages. The entire city of Reykjavik is heated by natural hot water, using a system gradually developed between 1930 and 1981 that has allowed the city to rid itself of coal and oil and accompanying pollution. The hot water was initially pumped in Reykjavik itself (one station is not far from the Hilton Nordica Hotel) but with the growth in population new pumping facilities were established further afield, near the lake at

Þingvellir, at Hellisheiði and on the way out of the city on the road to Hveragerði. In 2012 Reykjavik Energy reportedly provided 74.7 million tonnes of geothermal water to Reykjavik and the surrounding suburbs and towns, heating 95 per cent of homes.

The first people to be fitted with geothermal central heating were so proud that they would often overheat their apartments to impress their visitors even though they were suffocating. Only lately, with hot water so cheap, have there been attempts to conserve energy through synthetic mineral wool insulation and double glazing. As Icelanders habitually take off their shoes when coming into a home, underfloor heating is popular—and clean socks obligatory. At first the hot water pumped from the ground was sent directly into central heating systems, but traces of silica blocked the pipes and the hot water that was used in kitchens and bathrooms had a strongly sulphurous smell. These drawbacks are now largely a thing of the past as at Nesjavellir, near the Þingvellir lake, cold water that has been heated by geothermal hot water emerging from the ground at more than 100°C is sent to Reykjavik. This water, having heated homes and offices, is then recycled at about 37°C to clean and de-ice pavements on certain roads and to clear garage entrances in residential districts.

No mother in Reykjavik would dream of telling her child not to waste water, and electricity is equally inexpensive, meaning that people generally leave the lights on in every room during winter. The average monthly electricity bill for a large house in Reykjavik was less than €25 per month in 2013 and public lighting is often over-generous, although street lights come on later these days as an economy measure.

Nature has also been harnessed in the form of woodland and trees. In 1950 the average height of an Icelandic tree was eight metres, but has doubled since. The idea that the country contains no trees is a persistent cliché and has led to the old joke that in Europe one is hurt by falling from but in Iceland by walking into a tree (because it is so unexpected). Until relatively recently, the only trees to be seen in Reykjavik were those in graveyards, but this was not always the case. According to the Icelandic Forest Service, "at the time of human settlement about 1140 years ago, birch forest and woodland covered 25-40% of Iceland's land area", a situation that changed with deforestation and repeated glaciations. Nowadays Reykjavik is in fact surprisingly wooded—to the point of comprising Iceland's closest thing to a forest—and its trees, which proliferate in residential streets and parks, play a crucial role in combating the wind.

The city's green appearance is man-made. Indigenous species such as birch and willow appeared in dwarf varieties, and with the growth of Reykjavik other species were imported from different continents that could resist the wind, survive hard frosts and tolerate salt-laden sea breezes. Three species finally passed the tests: the black cottonwood from North America (imported in 1944) and the Siberian larch and willow. The dream of having big trees was realized but it contained seeds of its own nightmare; before 2000 nobody pruned the trees and it was forbidden to cut down a tree taller than four metres. The rampant roots of the black cottonwood now spread through drains and even threaten the foundations of buildings. The willows hide the sun and block many residential views, leaving many in Reykjavik cursing their obtrusive presence.

Church at Reykjavik (J. Ross Browne, *The Land of Thor*, 1867)

2

The Urban Map
Growth and Development

The Vikings, in the ninth century or perhaps even before, had settled in the bay (*vík*) of smoke (*reykur*). Before arriving in Iceland they had little or no experience of geothermal phenomena and naturally assumed that the steam escaping from the hot springs was smoke. Reykjavik, or Smoky Bay, is thus something of a paradox for the name of a capital that is so unpolluted.

Where Túngata meets Aðalstræti remains of ancient construction have been confirmed by Carbon-14 dating, but we know little more about the precise date of the earliest colonization. There were certainly significant and attractive resources: a river rich in fish and a lake full of birds as well as offshore islands where cereals could be grown. But the colonizers' boats went unreplaced, perhaps due to lack of wood, the links with Norway faded away and for centuries Reykjavik hibernated, for in reality it was at the centre of nothing and nowhere—the parliament was at Þingvellir and the bishops at Skálholt in the south and Hólar in the north. Reykjavik was a mere village, a situation that changed little during Danish colonization when the governor was at Bessastaðir, nowadays a suburb of the capital, but then simply a large and ramshackle settlement in the countryside.

It was in the eighteenth century that Reykjavik began to take shape when the title of *kaupstaður* or municipality was conferred on it. The first street to be paved was Aðalstræti in 1752, while warehouses, factories and basic housing grew up around it. It was also at that time that Iceland underwent a series of calamitous events with unusually violent volcanic eruptions decimating the population. The impact of the Laki eruption of 1783 was felt throughout Europe where a thick cloud of ash had a disastrous effect on crops and is even credited with contributing to the popular disaffection that led to the French Revolution. In Iceland the population declined dramatically as livestock was destroyed and hunger reduced the number of Icelanders to around 40,000.

Yet conditions improved in the nineteenth century. The only visual records we have of Reykjavik then are the drawings made by French, English or German visitors in order to convey the exotic reality of Iceland in their native countries—a daily reality that understandably did not much interest the small number of Icelandic artists. But how far we can rely on these depictions is open to debate. The French artist Auguste Meyer, who came in 1836 with an expedition sent by King Louis-Philippe, rendered the mountains of Iceland in Alpine style in order "to look more real" and when he drew the sheep he saw he added a shepherd, a detail unknown in Iceland where the sheep look after themselves.

Meyer depicts a scene of joyous activity in the streets of Reykjavik. Nowadays, thanks to tourists, to heated terraces and to impenitent smokers ejected by the law from the cosy torpor of the interior, the capital's streets have become lively again. We are forced to imagine the Reykjavik of the nineteenth century, however. Horses would have filled the streets, while fish dried on rocks near the sea (before it had access to salt Iceland used to export "stockfish", dried and cured fish). Water carriers would have been busy between the fountain and private homes, and farmers would make their yearly visit into town to buy basic supplies and might end up turning a year's hard work into glasses of aquavit consumed in a café-grocery store. However small it was, the capital was still a capital, defined by its function as much as its population, and people came from far and wide to enjoy a certain anonymity. Nineteenth-century Reykjavik was a Danish colony, and the Danish flag flew on Lækjargata, while the names of the shopowners were Danish: Fischer, Duus, Thomsen, Andersen, Zoëga, Isaakson or Jacobsen.

French Connections

Reykjavik is a port, but primarily a fishing and trading port, and even today it only takes the crew of one foreign military ship to completely change the town's atmosphere. It is not hard to imagine that in the nineteenth century the people of Reykjavik would have been delighted to see foreign fishing crews coming ashore to relieve the everyday monotony of their isolated lives. Not that we should underestimate the importance of the cod wars, the last of which against the British came to an end in 1976, but the nineteenth-century fishermen were not in trawlers, but fished from sailing boats with line and hook.

The most conspicuous fishing fleet, whose expeditions lasted several months, were the French, and they were in such numbers around Reykjavik that it is possible to speak of a French period like there was an English period before and after. Foreign fishing crews were only allowed to land in order to take on fresh water and to wash, and so that they could freely reach their consulate this was built at the seaside. The French consul M. Brillouin, married to a Norwegian woman, built a Norwegian-style Art Nouveau residence, Höfði, but had it decorated with symbols of the French Republic. On landing, according to diplomatic convention, the fishermen were thus on French soil. This house, where today the Reykjavik municipality holds its formal receptions, went on to enjoy a colourful history. It was subsequently bought by the British consulate but the resident ghost apparently prevented the consul from sleeping and it was sold again to the poet Einar Benediktsson, a great literary figure, lawyer and a mercurial businessman who eventually went bankrupt. He had grandiose plans, and opened offices in London where he sought foreign investment to exploit touristic interest in Iceland's aurora borealis or Northern Lights (and in doing so unwittingly invented virtual tourism, as what could be more intangible than the aurora borealis?). In 1986 Höfði played host to the high-level meeting between President Ronald Reagan and Mikhail Gorbachev that is considered a turning-point in the process of post-Cold War détente.

The French had also constructed a hospital (today a music school) on Frakkastígur, French Street, where the nursing staff was comprised of Catholic priests who agreed not to discuss religion with any locals who went there for treatment since the Icelandic parliament, still under Danish control, only granted religious freedoms in

1874, under pressure from the colonial power. There was, however, a Catholic chapel at Landakot, where the Catholic cathedral stands today. Mass was celebrated in the presence of a handful of ship-wrecked sailors or invalids awaiting repatriation, and a policeman on sentry duty ensured that no citizens could gain access to the chapel.

The survivors of shipwrecks had to be accommodated, and dormitories looking out onto both Austurstræti and the parliament building were constructed for this purpose until the heavy drinking of Breton fishermen ended in the building being destroyed. The huge wooden Hótel Ísland, containing several restaurants including the Svínastía (or "Pigsty"), was built at around the same time and was also notorious for its alcoholic excesses until it burnt down in 1944. But Bacchus, it seems, watched over the place, and when it became a car park it was baptized Hallærisplanið or Dead-End Square and in the 1970s was where some of the city's younger inhabitants used to drink a mix of homemade firewater and soda in the backseats of cars, thus perpetuating the tradition.

There was only one item—alcohol aside—that the Breton fishermen wanted to buy in a town that was far from anywhere and which had almost nothing—matches. Sold only in state tobacco outlets in France and subject to heavy taxation, matches were freely available in Iceland. They also swapped alcohol and hard biscuits for gloves, hats and other woollen items, and the more sober among them would save up their daily ration (two litres of wine and 25 centilitres of spirits) for trading. They became the stuff of legend in Iceland, not least among naughty children who were told that they used the flesh of red-headed boys and girls to bait their hooks. In fact, they endured terrible conditions and often died on board of tuberculosis (which at least brought their families a small pension). The sides of the sailing ships were very low and the risk of being thrown overboard ever-present; half of those who died were under sixteen years old.

Yet the fishing industry was profitable, and we have seen how the French planned a fish-drying factory in the north-east that would have had a population of 5,000 workers until British diplomatic pressure outweighed Danish support and the *Althing* rejected the plan.

Nineteenth-century Visitors

The golden age of travel, the nineteenth century, saw explorers and writers departing from Europe for all corners of the globe in search of the different and the exotic. The extremes of geography and culture were what attracted—the Far East, the Far North, etc.—but Iceland was perhaps not far enough north and yet also too isolated to appeal to romantic visitors. Islands were always a magnet, but Iceland was more like a small continent than an island idyll, with only a handful of smaller islands such as Grímsey or Heimaey acting as empty outposts in a cold and distant archipelago.

Nineteenth-century travellers were also in search of peoples with strange customs and religious beliefs, and they tended to precede, accompany or follow colonial occupation. But Iceland offered little colonial interest and had been a Christian land since 1000 AD. Its fascination lay in the fact that it was the living continuation of a Viking society that was all the more alluring because almost nothing was recorded from its past. Aside from a handful of jewels and other artefacts there was almost nothing and those who needed a visual representation of the Viking era in Iceland had little other than the Bayeux Tapestry, which represents William the Conqueror as part of a caste descended from the Vikings that had long since abandoned Norse for French. Such was Iceland's status at the time: a dried fish-exporting country with links to Denmark and Scotland. Beyond that little was known about it.

The French naval surgeon Joseph-Paul Gaimard and the writer Xavier Marmier undertook an expedition to Iceland and Greenland in 1835 and 1836. Gaimard was already an experienced traveller and natural observer, and this expedition was both scientific and literary as well as iconographic as Gaimard was to publish a twelve-volume work of which three were atlases containing over 200 lithographic plates based on the drawings of Auguste Meyer. The plates were sold separately in Iceland and their huge popularity had a lasting impact on how Icelanders viewed their own country and culture. Even if

Meyer decided to add tails to Icelandic sheep where they had none, his images are generally reliably accurate, and it could be claimed that he invented Iceland's visual past in the eighteenth century like Van Gogh invented that of Provence, which now strives to resemble the landscapes created in his paintings.

Gaimard had precise instructions, a long list of questions to answer and a group of scientists on board to assist. The National Academy of Medicine in Paris, for instance, asked him to provide an exact description of Icelandic women's genitalia. Curiously, while the French were prepared to go to Iceland in search of a complete manuscript of the story of Tristan and Isolde (due to the Norwegian monk Robert who had translated it into Norse) because the versions by Béroul and Thomas had gaps, they suspected at the same time that Icelandic "natives" might represent a different sub-species of humanity. In any event, Gaimard did not return empty-handed, bringing back a superb tapestry that is still kept in the Louvre as well as a fine specimen of an Icelander whom he showed off in polite society. The Icelandic writer Benedikt Gröndal has depicted the tragic end of this poor anthropological trophy who died falling from a balcony in Naples, and Gröndal offers two versions of this event: seeing Vesuvius he may have suffered from sudden home sickness and promptly killed himself; or due to an addiction to absinthe he may have lost his balance and slipped to his death.

Gaimard and Marmier also brought back potatoes from Iceland which when planted in France quintupled in volume. When the epidemic of potato blight devastated crops across Europe, leading to famine and mass migration, a rumour spread that the Icelandic tubers had resisted the disease and the Danish authorities wrote to Marmier to enquire whether he had any potatoes left. It was further evidence of how little contact existed between the colonial power and its colony.

The French doctor Henry Labonne travelled twice to Iceland in 1886 and 1887 on a mission supported by the Ministry of Education, with the aim of collecting botanical samples and animal specimens for Paris' Museum of Natural History. He was also instructed to study the commercial potential of exploiting sulphur and Iceland spar, a form of the mineral calcite—a strange task in hindsight given that sulphur has no value nowadays and is indeed the main obstacle to the geothermal industry in Iceland today. Labonne had reached the island like many travellers on the steamer *Camoens* which linked Leith in Scotland with Reykjavik and stayed at the Hotel Alexandra, even though the Hótel Ísland was more comfortable because he could not bear to be among so many British tourists.

Labonne was also a very good photographer, and Æsa Sigurjónsdóttir has reproduced some of his images in her beautiful book *L'Islande en vue*. Her book gives the impression that Labonne was cautious with his money, travelling around with his camera and constantly complaining about the difficulty of developing his photographs. It was, it seems, hard to find a suitable darkroom in Reykjavik, especially as he could not safely conceal himself and his developing equipment in a room that had no locks. He hired the schoolteacher Þorgrímur Guðmundsen as a guide—locals, then as now, had more than one job—and tried to reduce his costs by taking and developing photos in return for free board and lodging. He would ask his hosts, as seemed natural to him, to stand in front of their house with their farm workers and servants as this was the practice in France, the number of servants proving the family's wealth and standing. But they refused, as family was the most important factor in Iceland and it was considered insulting to be photographed next to servants. Labonne concluded in his book that class differences in Iceland must be considerable.

Another Frenchman who wrote about Iceland never actually set foot there. The heroes of Jules Verne's 1864 *A Journey to the Centre of the Earth*, we have seen, imagines his heroes descending into Snæfellsjökull's crater to reappear from Stromboli near Sicily (the Icelandic translator of the novel, fearing that his readers would not have heard of Stromboli, replaces it with Etna). An academic study has analyzed all the mistakes made by novelists who situated their novels in Iceland, and Verne emerges as the clear winner with not a single error. The armchair traveller may not have visited but he conscientiously used all available sources. Reykjavik, as described by Verne's narrator, appears as a poor, dismal little town but the description is doubtless faithful to the reality:

> In three hours I had visited not only the town but the surrounding areas. Its general appearance was particularly sad … During my tour I came across few inhabitants. On returning from the main commercial street I saw the greater part of the population busy drying, salting and loading cod, the main export article. The men seemed robust, but heavy and thoughtful, like blond Germans who feel themselves to be outside the mainstream of humanity, poor exiles cast out into this frozen land where nature might as well have made them Eskimos as it condemned them to live on the edge of the polar circle …

The female traveller E. J. Oswald was more complimentary, however, and her 1882 account, *By Fell and Fjord*, gives some indication of how Reykjavik was developing in the latter part of the century:

> The houses are, however, generally neat inside, and some of them are daintily pretty; and they are usually ornamented by roses, carnations, and geraniums, blooming in the windows, tender favourites which are rarely exposed to the open air. There are a few old turf-houses, which are among the worst and smallest specimens of the genuine Icelandic *bær* dwelling; and of late many new substantial houses of grey whinstone have been built. The red Danish flag flutters from many a roof, and the whole place has a thriving air, and an increasing trade and population.

British and Americans

Icelanders have an extremely complex relationship with Britain: encompassing admiration, fascination but also an element of rancour. The desire to be recognized and the dream of succeeding are stronger when it comes to their large neighbour than with other countries, even the Danes to whom they are so close. Yet to speak of "links" between Iceland and Britain is misleading because there is little in the way of reciprocity. If Icelanders know a good deal about Britain and have often been there, they are disappointed to find people there who have never heard of Iceland and cannot even name its capital. It is a stroke of luck if a map of Europe manages to include Iceland, and so to be Icelandic abroad is to run the risk of obscurity or even non-existence—hence an inferiority complex and a sense of frustration that some Icelanders can barely conceal when singing the praises of the country.

From Iceland at any rate there is a perceived proximity; the islands of the North Atlantic from Scotland northwards share a similar maritime culture and a culture of rain, mild winters and cool summers. Seen from Iceland—and everything depends on the point of view—Britain is a pleasantly temperate and sunny country where the visitor might go for a little warmth.

From the mid-sixteenth century onwards Iceland had, by contrast, had its share of problems: recurrent mini-Ice Ages, the loosening of its ties with Denmark and a governmental vacuum, a series of volcanic eruptions. If on the plus side there was plenty of land (and some historians now believe that Icelanders were no worse off than other Western European nations), there was worse to come when Iceland's rulers, already presiding over a more rigorous Lutheran Protestantism than that found in Denmark, forbade both the sale of alcohol and the presence of dogs in Reykjavik. There was little fun to be found in Iceland.

It took the arrival of the British and then the American military afterwards for Iceland to emerge wealthy from the Second World War and to mark the beginning of a period of prosperity. The British "invasion" took place on 10 May 1940 when a force of 746 marines disembarked in Reykjavik, to be followed a week later by 4,000 troops. The Allies were afraid that Nazi Germany, which had already occupied Norway and Denmark, would also seize Iceland and use it as a base to attack Allied shipping in the North Atlantic. Ignoring neutral Iceland's refusal to join Britain in the war, Winston Churchill planned the invasion in London and the expeditionary force encountered no resistance from either locals or the German crew of a shipwrecked freighter recently rescued by an Icelandic trawler. The authorities in Reykjavik protested that the territory's neutrality had been "flagrantly violated", but promises of compensation, political non-interference and eventual withdrawal restored calm.

At its height the British occupation involved some 25,000 military personnel, but within a year the British had been replaced by US forces, which eventually numbered 40,000. The majority of these were stationed in and around Reykjavik and their impact on the city, whose population in 1940 was estimated at 38,000, was immense. Employment boomed, while shops and restaurants were opened to cater to the American troops. The roads were properly surfaced, while cars, American for the most part, invaded Reykjavik. W. H. Auden, returning to Iceland after the war, talked to a former guide: "I asked him what life had been like during the war. 'We made money,' he replied" (*Letters from Iceland*). The Americans, for their part, were cold and bored. When the troops left—and some 1,500 remained to form the US-commanded Iceland Defense Force as part of Iceland's membership of NATO from 1949—they bequeathed a mixed legacy. The capital and surrounding areas were dotted with Nissan huts and other military infrastructure, while many locals had earned enough money to fuel the post-war building boom.

Liaisons between US troops and local women were commonplace and many children were born some of whom were given the patronymic *Hansson* (*hans* means "his" in Icelandic) because the father was unknown or had left the country. Mass consumerism arrived in the form of US tastes and pastimes. Social life changed, too. Hitherto it had been customary to walk around the town, dropping in on friends for a coffee, but the appearance of the driving *rúntur* (a hard-to-translate idea, literally "round tour" but now meaning pub crawl) changed urban habits. Girls would walk in pairs and arm in arm, ignoring the comments made by boys and hoping to see someone they knew behind the wheel of a car. Young people cruised around Reykjavik and met friends who got in and out of each other's vehicles, opting for the warmth of a car over the blizzard outside, but for the town it was a catastrophe. One café closed after another during the 1960s, and in Kvosin, the central area where parliament is located, the last shut in 1975. The city became dead at night.

There were dances held in big halls in town but situated far from the main residential areas. The queues to get into these gatherings were interminable, but bottles would change hands, warm hearts and break down inhibitions. The dance halls attracted hundreds of people, who were proud to go out and get drunk—something that is frowned upon today. In the 1970s young Reykjavikers had nowhere to go before they reached the legal drinking age of twenty and so would congregate in their thousands in the streets and squares of the capital where they drank illicit alcohol mixed with Coca-Cola. With no public toilets, boys and girls alike would urinate in alleys behind the houses in a spectacle that was primitive and innocent at the same time.

At the same time the disintegration of the oldest houses gathered pace. Their owners often rented them cheaply to the least desirable of tenants and were pleased when they were destroyed by fire, which happened all too often. The municipal authorities had a hand in the process. The conservative mayor, Davíð Oddsson, later to become prime minister and one of the main architects of the economic crash, was seemingly ashamed that buildings in central Reykjavik were less than five storeys high and hence not "modern", ignoring the fact that low-level homes are central to the city's charm and that tall buildings worsen the impact of high winds and prevent nearby homes from receiving what little sunlight there may be. In 1985 the city's authorities were still planning to demolish 29 old houses. This was Reykjavik's planning nadir; the city could only see better days.

A change in the municipal government, the election of a mayor open to urban restoration and finally tourism combined to save the town from demolition. The legalization of beer sales, outside heating and an influx of thirsty tourists have given it new life. Reykjavik is now a lively and living capital, with a plethora of cafés and restaurants and people always on the streets. Even when the weather is dreadful the smokers provide a minimum amount of outside life.

Nobody today really misses the days when one had to wait half an hour to be let into a dancehall. Reykjavik today is much more relaxed and convivial than it was forty years ago. And yet then, paradoxically, there was much more social mixing than now, when each social group finds its own exclusive place to meet. The atomization of the city's social life into many different venues, however pleasant it may be, also reflects the splitting up of society at large. Nowadays anyone who goes out for a meal or a drink is much more unlikely than before to come across people from a different social milieu.

Modern Growth

Demographic pressures and rural emigration led to tens of thousands of people moving into Reykjavik from the 1970s. New districts were built: Árbær, Breiðholt, then Grafarvogur, Gafarholt and Norðlingaholt. Contrary to what happens in other European cities, there was no real distinction between living in upmarket districts on the one hand and poorer areas on the other, even if the central 101 postal code confers a certain prestige. What social divisions exist occur within districts themselves, where the wealthiest live in detached houses, the moderately well-off in terraces and the least prosperous in apartments. The conservative politicians in power in Reykjavik until the end of the twentieth century favoured the privatization of property (85 per cent of families own their homes) and this was one of the causes of the domestic debt crisis that followed the financial crash. The new districts are well equipped with schools, sports facilities and shopping centres. Yet sometimes they have encountered teething problems, as in the case of Breiðholt, where a classroom in a primary school had to take in three groups a day—morning, midday and afternoon, as there were so many young children.

The city's new suburbs have improved with age, landscaped with many trees—friends and enemies of humanity since they protect from the wind but create unwelcome shade. Sociologically they have changed little in three decades apart from the fact that foreigners have tended to replace Icelanders in the privatized social accommodation.

For centuries Reykjavik turned its back on the sea, with only fish processing factories and warehouses along the coastline. New building techniques and the adoption of foreign architectural models have changed that tradition, and now it is fashionable to live on the tenth floor of a seaside apartment block where spacious verandas have replaced modest balconies with splendid views of mountains and water. There is always something to see: the play of light and darkness on the Esja range, the view that stretches a hundred kilometres to Snæfellsnes, the little fishing boats leaving port in the morning, the heavily laden returning trawlers and the huge cruise ships that can no longer fit into the old port and dock at Skarfabakki, five kilometres away.

The waterfront at Sæbraut now resembles many other redeveloped modern city areas, with condominiums, large roads, shopping districts and office buildings. The corporate and banking world, constrained by limited city centre office space, moved into this new district by the sea, with tower blocks as high as its ambitions. Seen from the sea or from Viðey across the water, Sæbraut is Reykjavik's Manhattan, and indeed in the years preceding the crash some dreamed of turning the city into a world financial hub, where a "world trade centre" was to be built next door to the planned new offices of Landsbanki and a new shopping and office complex. None of this saw the light of day, and all that remains of the dream is an immense open space in front of the Harpa concert hall.

The Island of Viðey: Imagine Peace

The island of Viðey, a few hundred metres from Reykjavik, is a historic, sacred and peaceful land. It abounds with birdlife, grass and soft hollows, combined with tranquillity and the spirit of bygone centuries. Some fine walking paths have been laid out on the island. The beach is a treasure for learning, experiencing and creating, and the difference between low and high tide is very marked. In the year 2006 a spot on the island was dedicated and consecrated for the so-called Imagine Peace Tower.

Viðey was first inhabited shortly after the settlement of Iceland and was the site of a major monastery in medieval times. During the eighteenth century it became home to the first governor of Iceland, Skúli Magnússon, who took up residence in the Viðeyjarstofa house. A printing press was later set up there, and in the early twentieth century the island boasted the country's most state-of-the-art dairy farm. The Icelandic state gave the island to the city of Reykjavik on the city's 200th anniversary in 1986, after which Viðeyjarstofa was renovated.

The Imagine Peace Tower stands on a platform seventeen metres in diameter, at the centre of which a light source emerges from a cylindrical "wishing well" four metres across and two high. The Tower is a work of art conceived by the legendary artist, musician and peace advocate Yoko Ono as a beacon to world peace and a memorial to John Lennon and is intended to project a strong and high column of light. It is lit every year from 9 October, Lennon's birthday, until 8 December, the date he was shot. The words "Imagine Peace" are inscribed on the well in 24 world languages. The electricity for the light comes entirely from Reykjavik Energy, which produces the electricity from geothermal power.

Viðey is a pleasant island to walk on and offers a different view of Reykjavik, but regular connections with the mainland are mainly confined to summer time. It is very peaceful, especially when the Imagine Peace programme is not going on.

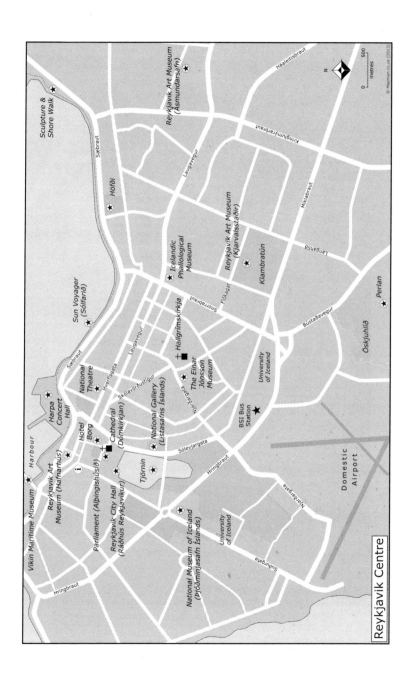

Reykjavik Centre

Sculpture & Shore Walk

Reykjavik Art Museum (Ásmundarsafn) ✪

Háaleitisbraut

N

0 500
metres

© Mapman.co.uk (2013)

Sæbraut

Höfði ✪

Laugavegur

Kringlumýrarbraut

Icelandic Phallological Museum ✪

Reykjavik Art Museum (Kjarvalsstaðir)

Miklabraut

Sun Voyager (Sólfariō) ✪

Sæbraut

Laugavegur

✝ Hallgrímskirkja ✪

Snorrabraut

Klambratún ✪

Flókagat

Langahlíð

Búastaðavegur

Perlan ✪

Harbour

Harpa Concert Hall ✪

National Theatre ✪

Hverfisgata

Skólavörðustígur

The Einar Jónsson Museum

Njarðargata

University of Iceland

Öskjuhlíð

Hotel Borg ✪

Cathedral (Dómkirkjan) ✝

National Gallery (Listasafns Íslands) ✪

Sóleyjargata

BSÍ Bus Station ★

Vikin Maritime Museum ✪

Reykjavik Art Museum (Hafnarhús) ✪

✪ i

Parliament (Alþingishúsið)

Tjörnin ✪

Reykjavik City Hall (Ráðhús Reykjavíkur)

Hringbraut

University of Iceland ✪

Domestic Airport

Njarðargata

National Museum of Iceland (Þjóðminjasafn Íslands) ✪

Suðurgata

Hringbraut

House in Hverfisgata (Christian Bickel/Wikimedia Commons)

3

Landmarks
Buildings and Styles

Reykjavik is a clean town where the air is pure and pollution-free. Its houses seem to have been painted only yesterday and its cars washed even more recently. The lawns are mown regularly, and bottles and cans are returnable for a deposit, meaning that down-and-outs collect them day and night and leave the streets free of litter. The ever-present wind blows any car fumes far out to sea. In short, Reykjavik appears to live up to its pristine tourist brochure image, and it sometimes seems that the only polluters are the seagulls and wild geese that like to leave their droppings around town. And yet the reality is perhaps not quite as perfect as the brochures make out. In winter studded car tyres scar potholes into the roads while an imperceptible chemical haze hovers over the melting snow. Nor is the atmosphere helped by the ash clouds from Eyjafjallajökull volcano that sometimes drift over the country.

Traditional Architecture

The first houses in Reykjavik had walls of volcanic basalt and peat, their roofs covered with thatch or turf. The centre of the house, used for cooking, had a hole in the roof through which smoke could escape. In the late eighteenth century a new form of house evolved in rural districts, the *burstabær*, with wooden ends or *gaflar*. Few such turf houses have survived, but the many museums of popular traditions contain authentic reconstructions.

Popular housing in eighteenth-century Reykjavik was mostly made of imported wood, while stone structures, designed and built by Danish craftsmen, were restricted mostly to churches and official buildings. Those homes constructed from volcanic rock were generally very modest in size and design, their walls rendered and now usually whitewashed with painted metal roofs.

Timber-framed buildings were largely prefabricated and imported from Denmark or Norway, with high pitched roofs and tarring to protect against the climate. J. Ross Browne in *The Land of Thor (1867)* painted a dismal picture of Reykjavik's wooden architecture:

A dark gravelly slope in front of the town, dotted with boats, oars, nets, and piles of fish; a long row of shambling old store-houses built of wood, and painted a dismal black, varied by patches of dirty yellow; a general hodge-podge of frame shanties behind, constructed of old boards and patched up with drift-wood; a few straggling streets, paved with broken lava and reeking with offal from the doors of the houses; some dozens of idle citizens and drunken boatmen lounging about the grog-shops; a gang of women, brawny and weather-beaten, carrying loads of codfish down to the landing; a drove of shaggy little ponies, each tied to the tail of the pony in front; a pack of mangy dogs prowling about in dirty places looking for something to eat, and fighting when they got it—this was all I could see of Reykjavik, the famous Icelandic capital.

This impression was echoed by the visitor Lord Dufferin four years later:

Reykjavik is a jumble of wooden shanties, pitched down wherever the builder listed. Some of the houses are painted white, the majority black, one has broken out in green shutters, another is daubed over with orange. The roofs are also of wood, and coloured black or grey. The town lies between the sea and a fresh-water lake full of reeds and wild-fowl; it is in the shape of a rude parallelogram, facing the sea on one side, showing its back to the lake on the other; the other sides rise up the slopes of hills from three to four hundred feet high, the one crowned by a windmill, the other by the Roman Catholic mission.

Not all wooden buildings at the time were slums; there were neoclassical and chalet-style homes for the rich and imposing government buildings and warehouses.

These prefabricated houses, sometimes ordered from catalogues and generally built by Norwegian contractors, offered infinite variety in terms of size and decorative features. Nonetheless they have sometimes proved to be poorly suited to Iceland's climate, which is less cold but windier than Norway. With no access to firewood, Icelanders had to burn coal then paraffin before technology brought thermal hot water for heating into the capital. Even so, it was essential to find a way of stopping the wind from getting between the wooden planks and creating freezing draughts. History does not record who invented the solution: fixing corrugated iron sheets to the outside of houses in the place of cladding, thus blocking wind and rain and creating a small pocket of air to encourage insulation and discourage humidity. The author of this example of architectural Darwinism remains anonymous, but Iceland's unique and practical response to its climatic challenges was born.

The main enemy of Reykjavik's wooden houses is not the woodworm, unknown in Iceland, but water which makes them rot. The oldest structures, built from wood that had grown slowly in the north of Norway and which had spent time floating in saltwater, are the toughest; those built in the inter-war period from unseasoned wood are the most vulnerable. The south-facing sides of houses, paradoxically, are more likely to be damaged by the climate than those facing north or west which rarely see the sun and are buffeted by the wind since the wind dries and drives away damp, while the sun is an infrequent and unreliable phenomenon.

The walls of many of the capital's houses are made of horizontal wooden planks separated by a gap of twelve to fifteen centimetres the width of the joists, which was traditionally filled with sawdust or even old woollen clothing. The exterior planks are clad in tar-lined paper, and very thin wooden battens onto which the sheets of corrugated iron are nailed provide a second space for insulation. Half a century ago a family with thirteen children might have lived in such a home, with a trade such as a blacksmith's forge located in the cellar.

The creaking of floors and ceilings creates a sense of promiscuity in these old houses, while the groaning of wooden walls during stormy nights or when the temperature suddenly changes led many in previous times to imagine a household ghost, the lost soul of a relative who was normally made welcome, joining the ten or more people already squeezed into the house. In order to create a minimum degree of sound insulation—for even the best behaved ghost can cause some annoyance when wandering around all night in the attic—Icelanders would often lay down several layers of flooring. The fashionable young couples who nowadays tend to restore old houses may smile condescendingly as they remove a layer of cardboard, another of linoleum and two of carpet from under the floorboards, but they later appreciate the logic of this multiple muffling technique when their young children begin playing in the attic room that they have cleared out for them in the hope of finding peace and quiet. Similarly accumulated layers of wallpaper, or even old newspapers, are found on walls.

With the comfort brought by unlimited hot water, cold is no longer an obsession, and today's house owners like to uncover and admire the warm-looking tones of the wooden interiors. When cement first appeared as a miracle material some of them tore off the rusting iron cladding and rendered their homes in cement—only to find that the wood soon rotted underneath the damp-conserving mortar.

But Iceland's contribution to world architecture is beyond any doubt the wooden house covered in corrugated iron. What in the rest of the world is a symbol of slums and shanty towns is in Iceland a work of art, its noble materials transcendent in the sharp light of winter. The material was originally imported from Britain in the 1860s, according to Adam Moremont and Simon Holloway in *Corrugated Iron: Building on the Frontier* (2007): "Ships travelling north from Britain to buy sheep would carry cargoes of corrugated iron to sell in Reykjavik, where it quickly became clear that the material was well suited to the isolated volcanic island with limited local construction materials."

Corrugated iron cladding has since become an art form in Iceland, often painted in bright colours especially near the port where the small houses boast the same paint and the same colours as the fishing boats. The wealthy homes of hillside Þingholt or those around the lake are more tastefully pastel but perhaps less spruce, but in any event fashions change. In the 1960s salmon pink and grey-green took over from pea green and ultramarine, while in the following decade anything went in Reykjavik as houses sported orange or even shocking pink exteriors. The 1980s, more discreet, favoured black and grey, with white recently coming into favour (white was previously confined to window frames as it is believed to minimize expansion and shrinking due to extreme changes in temperature). From 2000 onwards pastels have been popular again, a sign of middle-class good taste among those who think themselves faithful to tradition. This trend reached its peak with the repainting of the old *Gullborg* fishing boat by the Maritime Museum a subtle pastel yellow despite the fact that boats like this traditionally sported the brightest of colours

Icelanders' greatest enemy is the cold—not that it is particularly extreme but more because they have tended to deny its existence and have developed a style of architecture that does not take it into account. Some people have adapted a lifestyle to fit with their climate, but Icelanders have preferred an architecture that simply refuses to acknowledge the weather—this is why, according to some, they are poets.

Restoration and Imitation

The boom that preceded the bust in the Icelandic economy was marked by a backward movement in terms of Reykjavik's architectural profile. Anybody could borrow easy money without deposit or security to buy a property, and builders and estate agents rushed headlong into the abyss. Blocks of apartments of doubtful architectural value were built for young home buyers, and most of these today stand unoccupied.

In terms of restoring older buildings, however, the result was different, again largely due to tourism. Architects restored old homes, recreating those that had disappeared or simply inventing new versions of traditional buildings. The results, as in the case of the Hotel Centrum, could be spectacular. Here the challenge was three-pronged: to preserve the remains of buildings dating from the earliest settlement, to protect a large structure whose oldest parts dated back to 1764, and to build a big hotel on the site. Glass roofs bring together in harmonious fashion the different buildings, original and reconstructed, while the basement contains a museum. The purists may have questioned the process of renovation, but it was necessary as a minimum of urban cohesion had to be achieved, and even if the method can seem artificial, it at least worked. What was needed was in a sense what Icelanders had done with their own language when confronted with political independence, replacing Danish words with Icelandic neologisms. In order to create a coherent old Reykjavik it was a question of filling in the holes, rebuilding old houses or creating replicas artificially.

The problem lay, and lies, in the building materials used. The advocates of demolition in the 1980s were seemingly ashamed of traditional styles and wanted to sweep them away. Today's restorers are less drastic but still wish to make changes, consciously or not, most notably replacing corrugated iron with external wooden cladding. It may be true that widespread use of corrugated iron began towards the end of the nineteenth century and came to an end in the mid-1920s, but it is this material that is specific to Icelandic architecture, and in abandoning its use the capital is seeing its old houses not destroyed but radically modified.

Parliament (*Althing*) and Stone Buildings

The first non-rendered stone buildings appeared in Reykjavik towards the end of the nineteenth century. The stone was available in the town itself from a local quarry and the Danes were adept at hewing stone into building blocks. An Icelander named Sverrir also had the idea of using chunks of basalt that had already been carved by nature into blocks that merely had to be cut to size. The prison on Skólavörðustígur, the first stone building, was constructed using this method.

A committee of five members of parliament was set up to choose the design of the current parliament building, completed in 1881. Icelandic architects advocated externally rendered buildings, but it was a reputed Danish architect, Ferdinand Meldahl, who was selected to create a structure that would emphasize the natural dignity of the grey basaltic rock known as dolerite. The Danish master builder, Bald, chose to use more regular blocks than those obtainable via Sverrir's method, and the stone he employed was easier to carve but also fragile and was inexorably deteriorating before modern techniques stopped its erosion.

The crown of King Christian X still sits on top of the building's central pediment but the two coats-of-arms that used to decorate the façade have been removed: one represented the codfish that had for a time appeared on Iceland's flag, while the other featured the three lions of the Danish monarchy. The Dómkirkjan cathedral and the parliament, of similar height and situated side by side, are perfectly in harmony, their modest dimensions testifying to the impoverished past of a small nation.

The parliament originally had an upper and lower chamber, and voting on legislation took place with the two houses combined. A constitutional reform has since merged the two into a single chamber and laws are approved after a third reading. When parliament reconvenes in autumn the president and members of government along with foreign ambassadors take part in a religious ceremony at the

Dómkirkjan, after which they process, led by the Bishop of Iceland, into parliament. The short route from cathedral to parliament has been subject to heavy security since the crisis of 2008, and if the parliamentarians do their best to maintain a dignified appearance they are likely to face jeers from bystanders.

Grjótaþorp

A walk through Grjótaþorp ("rock village"), the oldest district of Reykjavik, reveals a large number of old dwellings. The area is encircled by the streets of Aðalstræti, Túngata, Garðastræti and Vesturgata, and these names immediately indicate our whereabouts as the word *straeti* is only used in the town centre. Starting at Aðalstræti, the paved square by the name of Ingólfstorg replaced Hallærisplanið (Dead End Square) in the mid-1990s; the former space had been the meeting place of Reykjavik's youth in the 1970s and 1980s. The buildings to the south are higher than the others, depriving the square of sun except in the height of summer. A pair of basalt obelisks support vents that sometimes send clouds of geothermal steam into the air, an arrangement that is meant to symbolize Iceland but perhaps might have been better served by a warm water fountain. Since its creation the square has had little raison d'être other than as a meeting place for skateboarders, and is scheduled to be redeveloped once more.

Aðalstræti, on its west side, is the street for city centre hotels: the Plaza, the Hotel Centrum and, a little further and less luxurious, the Salvation Army Guesthouse. Tourists keep this road busy, winter and summer and whatever the weather. Between the tourist office and the Plaza Hotel is Fischerssund, a small street that for a long time had different spellings at either end, as at the bottom the genitive "s" had been left off the street sign. It is apparent that the street name, in honour of the Danish trader Fischer who used to occupy the present tourist office, is not easy to spell. Around 1900 a policeman discovered a corpse here and got out his notebook to record the time and place. But when he was about to write the name of the road he hesitated—to make a spelling mistake seemed so dreadful that he dragged the body to Veltusund, two streets away, to fill in his report. I have never heard of a greater tribute to the Icelandic language.

To the right is the Geysir Bistro restaurant, while on the left is the Plaza, which has integrated older buildings into its layout and was once the premises of a ship-owner who dried cod before the Second World War. Cases of *kaffibætir* or "export", roast chicory for coffee production, were then stored here during the war, but at the end of the conflict when consumption of coffee substitutes declined the building was turned into a boarding house. Next came a chemist, and there were soon queues of alcoholics waiting until the shop opened at 9 a.m. to buy supplies of 90° proof spirits; the Grjótaþorp area was littered with empty plastic bottles of pharmaceutical spirits. (When the chemists in turn closed it was always possible, as a final resort, to buy small bottles of vanilla-flavoured rum extract for cake-making from a grocery.) The chemist moved away, got rid of its old staff and moved into a new shopping centre. It was succeeded by a shop that sold aquariums and fish, then by a pub called Duushús where Björk and her band the Sugarcubes performed for French president François Mitterrand and President Vigdís Finnbogadóttir in 1991. The pub gave way, rather less festively, to an undertaker's office and then to a nightclub baptized Clinton—"cigars a speciality", claimed its advertising. As female dancers gyrated in front of mirrored columns the place was engulfed in controversy, especially as the feminist movement had raised money to buy a group of houses opposite. In the end, the business failed and the premises were acquired as an annex by the Plaza Hotel. In its heyday it was called the "Liverpool" building, and the small space in front of it is named Glasgow planið (Glasgow Square) in memory of the house of that name which once stood here. A little further is the Aberdeen house, painted bright red, which was owned by the poet and businessman Einar Benediktsson.

To the left going up Fischerssund where the street meets Mjóstræti is the strangely named Norwegian Bakery—neither Norwegian nor a bakery, but a wooden house dating from 1876 owned by a writer who was also a filmmaker and member of parliament. Across Mjóstræti two houses called Hildibrandshús and Hákot stand opposite each other in the narrow pedestrian-only extension. A peasant and fisherman lived in Hákot and in 1901 built for his only daughter a wooden house on the other side of the passage. She was married to the son of a French fisherman with whom she had thirteen children, while he shoed horses in the cellar, only zinc sheets protecting the wooden house from his forge. The thirteen children, meanwhile, spent much of their lives outside the house, especially as the family rented part of it to lodgers.

Returning to Mjóstræti, we come across the "poets' path" leading to the red-painted Unuhús, a gathering point for artists and intellectuals in the early twentieth century where the writers Halldór Laxness and Þórbergur Þórðarson used to go for coffee. Vinaminni at Mjóstræti 3 is unusual by Reykjavik's standards for its very high ceilings (its owner had lived in Italy), and during the 1970s it had several tenants from France. Almost a third of the district's houses had been bought up by the owners of a chain of minimarkets who hoped to make a handsome profit when the authorities knocked them down to make way for a new major road. The plan never materialized, however, the neighbourhood fell into disrepair and the remaining speculator, who had become slightly confused in his old age, became convinced that only French tenants paid their rent— which was probably true.

The street leads to a small square with a children's seesaw, the place where Laufey Jakobsdóttir, the so-called "grandmother of Grjótaþorp" and an advocate of women's and children's rights, used to offer much-needed weekend toilet facilities to the capital's inebriated and distressed youth. The toilets have since been destroyed, but a near-by plaque commemorates Sigvaldi Kaldalóns (1881-1946), one of Iceland's most celebrated composers. The municipal authorities were so ashamed that the great man was born in a poverty-stricken little hovel that the plaque was placed some way away from his actual birthplace. The hovel has since been rebuilt and transformed at huge expense into a bijou residence that has nothing to do with the original, and the plaque has still not been moved.

Coming down Brattagata towards Aðalstræti, the blue house on the right was built for the Jewish guide Zoëga, whom William Morris employed along with his horses. Morris also acquired his provisions at Fischer's establishment on Aðalstræti.

Reykjavik's conservationists were unsuccessful in saving the Fjalakötturinn ("mousetrap") house on this street, where hit shows were performed during the Second World War. The building's main room had previously been a cinema, and it is even claimed that it was the first cinema in the world, showing films from 1906 onwards. This is only partly accurate, as the earliest films were always screened in theatre halls in Iceland because of the weather whereas elsewhere in Europe they were often shown in fairground booths. The building was controversially demolished in 1985.

For the most part, however, Grjótaþorp's houses have been well restored, even if those nostalgic for the past complain that there is no longer washing hanging out to dry or dandelions flowering in neglected corners. In the 1980s the area was mainly home to tenants, all of whom were forced to move when the properties were sold. Those who feared that their houses would disappear, as had been ordained, may today be happy that they were saved. Locals and visitors can walk around the district's streets at any time of year, as the city's thermal heating and drainage system allows warm water to be collected from homes and recycled to keep streets free from snow.

Modern Architecture

Iceland boasts a very large number of architects. Some cynics suggest that they proliferate because students only receive grants to study abroad if their chosen subject is not taught in Iceland—which is the case with architecture.

Even if Reykjavik's contemporary architecture can often look like that to be found anywhere else—and is a far cry from the nineteenth-century fashion for corrugated iron—it still has its own distinctive features. First, there is space. Land is not in short supply and the new neighbourhoods are separated from the road network by generous green spaces. Gardens are large, even in the centre of town, and children can often play in the street. In Reykjavik it is sometimes easy to imagine that one is in the country until in the winter evenings the entire conurbation is bright with street lights and it seems, especially looking down from the hills, that it is a vast metropolis. If Reykjavik remains a green city, the reverse is that such a spread-out urban area makes public transport very difficult to organize.

Iceland has been subjected to series of external influences. Denmark was long the point of reference for prestigious projects such as the parliament building or the *Safnahúsið*, the first purpose-built national library (1906), but the functionalism that flourished between the wars also had a Danish imprint. Imitation was restricted, however, by the fact that the main building material used in Denmark—bricks—was by and large unavailable and imports would have been prohibitively expensive. The same obstacle curtailed British influence, which was limited in the post-war period to the semi-cylindrical corrugated-iron military huts that were lived in once the troops had left. A cinema, Hafnarbíó, even opened for business in one of the prefabricated barracks.

After the Second World War American tastes prevailed in the form of houses and apartment blocks built with flat roofs, which invariably leaked. The architects had underestimated the climate and in the 1970s pitched roofs returned, even in apartments. The luxury villa appeared towards the end of the century, often in *nouveau riche* neoclassical or mock Hispanic style. In the years preceding the financial crash a spectacular property boom encouraged many Icelanders to buy new property for letting, and thousands of Polish and Baltic workers were accommodated in these same new developments. By 2008 Reykjavik was a forest of construction cranes, an unmistakable sign, said some economists, that a crash was inevitable. And so it was.

Modern Icelandic architecture has developed with little connection to the surrounding climate, with cheap heating discouraging any adaptation to the environment. Houses that one might expect to see in Florida or California are an implicit protest against the climate by a people who have never got used to it. The interior of Reykjavikers' homes counts for more than the exterior which is often uninspiring with its double garage doors, though the back façade may be more luxurious—a very Protestant rejection of ostentation. That ostentation is to be found in the luxury cars parked outside while the garage houses the snowmobile or the table tennis unless it has been turned into an apartment.

Another constant theme in local architecture is the search for materials that will resist wind, rain and salt. After the period of corrugated iron came a phase when crushed seashells were mixed into plaster to create pebbledash, followed by various metallic exteriors. Nowadays glass, which prettily reflects the capital's ever-changing skies, is in favour.

The City Hall

Although Reykjavik's council offices were for many years scattered throughout the city, the decision to build a new city hall by the

City Hall (Tupungato/Shutterstock)

Tjörnin lake was controversial. After an international competition, it was designed by the Icelandic-British Studio Grandi firm (which then went on to design the modernist Supreme Court building), and opened in 1992 with the offices of the mayor and exhibition spaces. Opponents of the project argued that the mostly nineteenth-century wooden houses around the lake presented an example of architectural unity that would be brutally disturbed by a concrete building. The "Tjörnin lifi" (Long live the lake) campaign then became part of a wider movement to conserve old buildings in the capital. The city hall was eventually built but the controversy surrounding it helped to raise consciousness of Reykjavik's architectural heritage and saved other buildings from demolition. The fountain made of gabbro rock is considered a success but the entrenched desire to import stones into such a mineralogically rich country may seem strange. Open to the public, the building contains a topographical relief model of Iceland, and a walkway allows visitors to observe the lake's abundant population of swans, geese, ducks and gulls. For generations young children have been brought here with bags of breadcrumbs to feed the birds.

Perlan

Situated on the Öskjuhlíð Hill overlooking the capital, the five giant storage tanks, built in the 1940s, contained geothermal hot water for distribution throughout Reykjavik. The overflow was pumped into the sea through an artificial stream that used to attract weekend visitors in search of relaxation or a hangover cure. In 1991, after the tanks were updated, it was decided to place a new hemispherical structure on top of them, creating a space age-looking arts centre with concert halls, a viewing gallery, shops and a revolving restaurant.

Designed by Ingimundur Sveinsson, Perlan ("The Pearl") was funded by the water company and at first critics condemned it as expensive and elitist. But it has been an enormous success, and Reykjavik's people have embraced the post-modern structure, flocking to have a drink or ice-cream in winter and summer. If the restaurant is rarely full, the cafeteria below, which opens out onto a terrace, is always busy and lively with Reykjavikers who come to make out their homes below with or without binoculars.

Centre or Suburb

Here are two property advertisements published on the same day, 9 January 2012. The first is for an apartment situated on Reykjavik's main shopping street, Laugavegur:

> Laugavegur, 101 Reykjavik. Very well designed apartment, 67m², 2 rooms on second floor in town centre. Windows and frames, exterior walls and wiring modernized. The apartment is available immediately. 19 million.

The second lists the attractions of an apartment in a block in a distant suburb. The block is charmless, and buses are few and far between in the suburb:

> Klukkurimi, 112 Reykjavik. Very attractive and bright apartment, 89m², 3 rooms on 3rd floor in a good-quality apartment block. Magnificent views, entrance hall, 2 rooms, kitchen, bathroom and lumber room on ground floor. Private parking. 19.9 million.

There are a few more square metres in the second advertisement, but it is a floor higher up with no lift. For the sake of comparison the first apartment is located, let us say, in Bond Street, the second in some far-flung suburb of London. Yet the difference in price is insignificant, as Icelanders do not as yet attach snob value to city-centre addresses. They are also dependent on their cars, and being able to park comes first. But the capital's traffic jams and the rising price of petrol are slowly starting to change attitudes.

Statue of Ingólfur Arnarson, "the first settler"
(TommyBee/Wikimedia Commons)

4 | Rulers and Ruled
A Brief Social and Political History

The first settlers, who are said to have arrived around 870, held *þing* or local assemblies each year, following a tradition solidly rooted in Norway, their land of origin. To settle disputes between regions or to gain approval of new laws they also created in 930 the *Alþing* or *Althing* (literally the "all-thing"), a general assembly of clan chiefs. Free men travelled in summer to the *Althing*, but only the 39 local chieftains, whose position was hereditary, took part in this legislative assembly whose rulings were recited by the *lögsögumaður*, "he who says the laws" or the lawspeaker, before being inscribed from the eleventh century on parchment. Its deliberations took place in the open air at Þingvellir in front of the great volcanic escarpment of Almannagjá with its unusually clear acoustics. The assembly also had at its disposal several tribunals and, for the first time, an appeal court with a jury. On the other hand, the *Althing*'s executive power was all but non-existent, with the local chiefs firmly in command. Those who were condemned to banishment had three years in which to flee, after which anybody was entitled to kill them.

The *Althing* met for a fortnight each year, during which clan leaders and poets alike would compete among themselves while their families set up encampments in the Þingvellir plain and set about carousing. Those returned from distant expeditions told stories and boasted, plots were hatched, alliances were formed and fates were sealed. Tradesmen and entertainers of all sorts were drawn to the assembly, setting up rudimentary turf and stone dwellings. Icelandic historiography has idealized this period. Family feuds, the judgements handed out by the *Althing*, the legal ramifications and acts of revenge fuelled the celebrated sagas. The landscape in which these events took place, spectacular with rocky outcrops and clear streams, has hardly changed since the first colonization.

It is difficult to say today whether this society was as egalitarian as has been suggested. It was perhaps true for as long as any free man had the right to claim the lands that he could cover by foot in one day. But by the thirteenth century, when the Sturlungar dynasty was imposing itself, Icelandic society was strongly reminiscent of a feudal system. Rival families attempted to seize power; internecine squabbles ruined parliament's credibility; a civil war precipitated the decline of this first republic. The country fell under Norwegian (1262), then Danish (1380), domination. The *Althing* somehow managed to survive that "long night" but its role was no more than judicial. By the eighteenth century the assembly's building was in such a state of disrepair that its archives blew away through ruined windows. The magistrate Magnús Stephensen announced that he would no longer officiate "in a cold draught" and would henceforth judge in Reykjavik. Plaintiffs were delighted as court sittings would now take place every fortnight in winter and weekly in summer, but the nation was in the process of losing its soul. The *Althing* was disbanded between 1800 and 1845, when it was reformed as a consultative body for the Danish Crown.

By the end of the eighteenth century the country, exhausted by famine, a virulent smallpox epidemic, the eruption of the Laki volcanic system (1783) and above all by despair, could sink no lower. But then came the reawakening, even the resurrection, of the nineteenth century, linked to the peaceful but resolute struggle in the name of democracy. The *Althing* was restored in 1845 with pressure from nationalist movements and partially re-established in its old duties. Secession, supported by the association of Icelandic patriots, was in motion.

If the Danes controlled Iceland's destiny for centuries, the British were also key players. One of several critical moments was at the time of the Napoleonic Wars (1803-15) when Denmark, which had sided with France, was cut off from its colony. It was Britain that dominated the seas and Britain that controlled maritime trade links with Iceland. In 1803 British ships carrying grain saved Icelanders from famine (even if 450 died of hunger in that year alone). The great explorer and scientist Sir Joseph Banks entertained the idea of invading Iceland, but the British had a longer-term strategic goal. Denmark emerged weakened from the Napoleonic Wars, but Sweden was strengthened. The country was led by Jean-Baptiste Bernadotte, a former Marshal of France and ally of Napoleon, who changed political sympathies at the right time. Now King Charles XIV, it is said that this former revolutionary had the slogan "death to the king" tattooed on his chest (he reportedly took care to bathe out of sight of his servants).

Sweden annexed Norway, lost by Denmark, and became a regional power. Britain realized that it needed to contain Swedish ambitions, and in 1814 the Treaty of Kiel stabilized the region. According to the historian Björn Þorsteinsson, Britain considered that Greenland, the Faroe Islands and Iceland should be under its protection and that in no circumstances should these strategically important territories fall into Sweden's orbit. A British presence at the negotiations ensured that though Sweden, which had lost Finland to Russia, demanded Norway as compensation, it would not win control of the three formerly Norwegian "vassal states", which Britain wished to remain under Danish rule.

History, normally indifferent to the fate of small nations, continued to shape Iceland's fortunes to the advantage of external interests. In 1918 it received autonomy from Denmark only because at the Treaty of Versailles the Danes, who had lost Schleswig-Holstein in 1864 to Prussia and Austria, insisted that should be a popular plebiscite to determine its future—and hence could hardly refuse the same democratic right to Iceland. Towards the end of the Second World War, the occupying American authorities were initially opposed to Iceland's independence, but changed their position as they realized that an independent state would be more grateful and malleable than a dependency of Denmark—at that point under Nazi rule.

This is perhaps not the official version of national history taught in schools—a succession of heroes, often poets, and a peaceful march towards independence—and it is not intended as an insult to Iceland to suggest another version of this history. Heroes there certainly were, but only seventy years after independence it is still too soon to analyze this history with objectivity.

Icelandic Nationalism

The stages of the struggle for Icelandic independence were, it is true, always peaceable. Born among a group of students in Copenhagen in the first half of the nineteenth century, Icelandic nationalism produced an abundance of poems but never resorted to armed conflict. Nothing in terms of religion, ethnic origin or culture in the broadest sense separated the Icelanders from the Danes, but the very fact of living on a remote volcanic island and still speaking the language that the colonizers themselves had spoken in the distant past was enough to underline the real differences. In 1845 the *Althing* was granted its consultative role, and in 1874 certain tax-raising powers were transferred followed by the end of the Danish trade monopoly and the introduction of a free press. All these reforms ran parallel to democratization in Denmark itself, including the Schleswig-Holstein pebiscite. The home rule statute, involving sovereignty in a union with the Danish Crown, was approved almost unanimously in a referendum, leaving one last stage to be reached: full independence. This was proclaimed in 1944 while Denmark was occupied by Germany, and was approved by the United States whose military had replaced that of Britain on Icelandic soil in 1941.

The emblem of the island, a codfish and a golden crown, gave way to the present-day blue, red and white national flag. The language was purged of many of its Danish neologisms and the people were given a national anthem that almost nobody nowadays knows how to sing. Today the *Althing*, the oldest existing parliamentary institution in the world, consists of 63 elected deputies and members of the public can attend its sittings without having to show proof of identity.

Political Parties

Since the Second World War Iceland's political system has more closely resembled that of Finland than any other Scandinavian country. Neither sociological revolutions, the collapse of the Soviet Union, the departure of the American military nor the weakening impact of electoral campaigns have altered the presence of four political parties, all of whom are willing to enter into coalition governments.

The most important of these is the conservative Independence Party (Sjálfstæðisflokkurinn), strongly rooted in the fishing industry, commerce and among the well-off middle class. The centrist Progressive Party (Framsóknarflokkurinn), once labelled agrarian, has survived the demise of the cooperative sector that it used to dominate and defends the interests of farming communities while espousing traditional values. Like the Independence Party, it is opposed to Icelandic accession to the European Union.

The Social Democratic Alliance is influential among the trade unions and governed in alliance with the Independence Party up to 2008 before leading a left-wing coalition from 2009 to 2013. It is the only party to favour joining the European Union. Its pro-American sympathies in a country where the presence of a NATO base was controversial have encouraged the presence of a fourth, more radical and nationalist, force. Communist in origin, this group embraced ecological politics and bears the name of the Left-Green Movement.

Of the four parties two are left-leaning and two centre-right or right-wing in policy, but two—the Social Democratic Alliance and the Independence Party—are open to the exterior and internationalist in outlook, while the Progressive Party and Left-Green Movement are more attached to old-fashioned national issues and values.

Women and Politics

With the exception of Freydís and other strong, determined and formidable individuals in the saga tradition, women are largely missing from the history of Iceland, and it is not until the twentieth century that they reappear. Previously there are conspicuously few tragic heroines, scheming mistresses or champions of emancipation, and as Iceland never had a queen there had been few women in positions of power. A Lutheran moral code also discouraged literary muses and prevented women from exercising influence from behind the throne.

But from the second half of the twentieth century Icelandic women rapidly made up for lost time. The *Rauðsokkur* or Red

Stockings, who were part of the social and ideological turbulence of 1968, developed a form of radical feminism, while non-feminist women's associations, strong in Protestant tradition, also became increasingly radicalized. In October 1975 these various groups organized the spectacular women's strike against low pay and other forms of discrimination, which brought together an estimated 25,000 women out of a total population of barely 220,000 in central Reykjavik. "The women were from all walks of life, young and old, grannies and schoolgirls; some wore their uniforms from work, others had dressed up," recalls Annadís Rúdolfsdóttir. While the women listened to speeches, men suffered with their new-found responsibilities: "Some went out to buy sweets and gathered pencils and papers in a bid to keep the children occupied. Sausages, the favourite ready meal of the time, sold out in supermarkets and many husbands ended up bribing older children to look after their younger siblings. Schools, shops, nurseries, fish factories and other institutions had to shut down or run at half-capacity."

The movement lived on with the creation of an exclusive women-only party, Kvennalistinn or the Women's Alliance, which disbanded in 1999 after making many of the gains that it had sought—before 1983 women accounted for only five per cent of deputies, but in 1995 this had risen to thirty per cent with several parties advocating a quota for women on party lists. The Alliance had also run out of steam and several of its leaders had become mainstream parliamentarians, no better and no worse than their male counterparts.

Vigdís Finnbogadóttir was the first woman to be elected head of state by universal suffrage. She beat three male candidates in 1980 without winning an overall majority, but was triumphantly re-elected on three further occasions. Cultivated and elegant, she was a professor of French and a theatre director before becoming a political icon. Yet her success was misunderstood abroad where it was thought that her election was a consequence of the women's strike and of the feminist movement. She insisted, however, that she was elected by the entire population, and by electing a divorced woman recovering from cancer Icelandic voters did indeed act as precursors in abandoning prejudices. She considered her main role to involve raising awareness of Icelandic culture, while her successor, Ólafur Ragnar Grímsson, saw himself as the international champion of the country's businessmen, jetting off to every opening of the Icelandic banks' subsidiaries—businesses that were doomed to bankruptcy.

Jóhanna Sigurðardóttir, president of the Social Democratic Alliance and a member of parliament from 1978, was prime minister from 2009 to 2013. Little is known about her private life, but her years as an air hostess, when she was active in expanding trade union rights, are well documented. She brought up two boys alone after a divorce while working in a cardboard box factory before entering into a civil partnership with Jónína Leósdóttir in 2002 and a same-sex marriage—one of the first in Iceland—in 2010. Some have criticized her as uncharismatic, but she was instrumental in steering Iceland through the turbulence of its worst-ever economic crisis, an achievement that in 2009 would have seemed miraculous. She announced her imminent retirement from politics in 2012.

The 2008 Crash

We will deal with the impact of Iceland's great economic collapse in later chapters and it is referred to in many other places in this book. Since it emerged from the Atlantic Ocean, Iceland has suffered a multitude of eruptions and earthquakes, but the crash of every bank in the country in 2008 was on a human Richter scale the strongest tremor ever recorded.

The Guardian's headline read: "The party's over for Iceland, the island that tried to buy the world", and the author of the piece continued: "the króna, Iceland's currency, is in freefall and is rated just above those of Zimbabwe and Turkmenistan." This moment marked the beginning of the full-fledged crisis, but its causes went back to 2003 and perhaps beyond. Nor is the crisis over, even if other countries' economic woes have since overshadowed those of Iceland.

The crash's origins have been thoroughly analyzed by economists and historians. First there was the reform of fishing quotas, which became sellable commodities, transferable and divided in two in the event of divorce. The traditional quota, an entitlement, was transformed into a financial asset that could be traded, and the resulting market in quotas flooded the economy with considerable amounts of money. Then came the privatization of the banks, mostly shrouded in corruption and scandal, as the process, due to political cronyism, was left in the hands of speculative businessmen—the "Nordic Tigers" or "New Vikings"—who never paid for the financial establishments that they acquired. The rest is well-known; in the hands of their amateur proprietors, Iceland's banks fuelled what was one of global capitalism's most surreal episodes.

It should be said that the present author, omniscient of course, a veteran observer of Icelandic society and probably no stupider than anyone else, failed to avoid losing his savings in the debacle. This is not to bemoan his bad luck but to show that Icelanders in Iceland were aware of very little as most of the dealings were carried out abroad.

Lack of foresight notwithstanding, it is now clear that there are two interrelated crises: the first surrounds relations between Iceland and the countries that lent it money; the second is an internal one, connected to the first, but in fact rather harder to resolve. What is at stake in the international context is how to negotiate repaying foreign creditors on the best available terms. The internal issue is one of managing the indebtedness of the Icelandic population, which has become increasingly critical due to the *króna*'s depreciation and the fall in the standard of living.

Icelanders learnt at the beginning of October 2008 that their country's banks had borrowed on international markets the equivalent of eleven times Iceland's GDP. International banks were happy to make the loans because Iceland was by all definitions a respectable and reliable country, a Protestant northern nation like other reputable Scandinavian states and with a triple-A rating from the credit agencies and a top ranking in world human development indices.

What happened to this money? It is estimated that at the time of the full-scale crash Icelandic banks owed approximately £50 billion (US$75billion). The sale of assets has enabled, and will enable, the banks to pay back some of these debts, but foreign lenders have suffered big losses, taken by surprise by what was the first international banking collapse. In many cases, too, they have kept quiet about it, preferring to keep their losses secret and selling their toxic assets to anonymous junk funds.

The banks that failed were resurrected and renamed almost the day after their collapse—or so it seemed. It also seemed that the crash might have turned out to be a good bit of business for some, although not for the average Icelander, for how else can one describe a situation where money that is borrowed is never repaid? Apart from Landsbankinn, which was nationalized, the new banks were owned and controlled by their foreign creditors, whose identity is not necessarily known. It is assumed that the reluctant owners will wish to sell the banks—but to whom? Of the biggest finacial crashes of recent years Salomon Brothers leads the way in terms of losses, but in the top ten there are three Icelandic institutions: Kaupþing (4th), Glitnir (6th) and Landsbankinn (10th).

Nobody trusts a country in financial freefall, and emergency measures were undertaken. The Central Bank's assets were frozen by government decree and the country looked for other countries likely to lend it money. The Scandinavian nations all refused, while Russia pretended to help if only to increase its influence. Iceland "lined up an increasingly desperate attempt to avoid financial collapse," observed Canada's *Globe and Mail*, not knowing that its efforts were useless. The IMF, more civilized since recognizing its past mistakes, finally offered Iceland a reasonable aid package, and the Scandinavians then agreed to lend via the IMF.

But in Iceland that was not the end of the story, as the people, embittered and anxious for the future, demonstrated against the government, a coalition of social democrats and conservatives. Icelanders of all ages and social backgrounds converged on the parliament building to beat saucepans and hurl fireworks and other missiles. At the beginning of 2009 Reykjavik witnessed its first violent street protests since the 1949 anti-NATO disturbances. The weakened government rapidly imploded, the two leaders of the coalition including Prime Minister Geir Haarde announcing their retirement due to illness. New elections were announced, which in

April brought to power the coalition of social democrats and the Left-Green Movement.

An Impoverished People

The average Icelandic salary fell in value by 21.5 per cent in 2008, 10 per cent in 2009 and 16 per cent in 2010. These figures are the logical consequence of the Icelandic *króna*'s devaluation, losing half its value against the euro within eighteen months of the crash. From one day to the next, in October 2008, one of their wealthiest peoples in the world became a nation in retreat, begging to be allowed to join the European Union in the vain hope of finding a degree of stability.

Yet Icelanders managed to adapt to their new situation, veering between lethargy and rage, depression and hope. What was wanted was a holding to account of those responsible for the financial tsunami that had transformed a small northern, Lutheran nation into the world's most indebted country. But it was also a period in which Iceland turned in on itself, looking for a new small-scale, sustainable lifestyle free of credit and conspicuous consumption. In Reykjavik conversation turned inevitably to the crisis, ranging across despair, hope that prosperity might return, regret at having been so naïve during the boom and anger against the culprits. People also felt guilty at having let things happen and bitterness towards Scandinavian countries that had done nothing to help. On the one hand it was hoped that those responsible would pay off their debts, but people also prayed that the debts contracted by the failed Icelandic banks would eventually be written off. Today Icelanders have various terms that are applied to the crisis. *Kreppa* means stagnation or recession; *hrunið* is the word that evokes the crash itself and is used to compare life before and after. The violent demonstrations that did away with the government are now known as the "kitchenware revolution" (*Búsáhaldabyltingin*), while a new expression has appeared meaning anything that is expensive, chic or luxuries—"very 2007".

Not everybody suffered equally from the crisis. In fishing villages far from the capital there was a state of near euphoria as fish sold in euros was bringing in twice as many *krónur*. Salaries were frozen but productivity continued unabated in a sort of revenge for the rural population who two years later thought it had missed the train of modernity.

As for the super-rich, they no longer lived in Iceland, but in Copenhagen or London or even in both from where they conducted their business long-distance. Angry youths daubed the 4×4s and villas of those who dared to return with red paint, and most wisely decided to stay abroad. They left behind the unfinished and very large building sites of their planned second homes as a memory of past ambitions.

The same delusions of grandeur haunted the centre of Reykjavik with the Harpa concert hall and the Congress conference centre under construction. The city authorities and the state finally decided to finance the completion of these works having considered leaving them unfinished as a memorial to the crash. Paid for by the people, these projects outstripped in both size and cost Ceausescu's presidential palace in Bucharest.

The middle-income inhabitants of Reykjavik (probably two-thirds of the population), meanwhile, cut back on everything and started paying off their debts, leaving the rich to renege on theirs. Automobile sales fell by 85 per cent in a year, kitchen appliances by sixty per cent. Things were made to last, and the better-off parted with their second or third car, many of which crossed the Atlantic to be resold in Europe. Allotments were suddenly popular again and dietary habits changed in a shift of identity as people resorted to such traditional and economical home-made staples as liver sausage and black pudding (the trend was temporary and most black pudding stayed in the freezer). McDonald's shut up shop in Iceland and in the process it was discovered that all its ingredients were imported from Germany. A new burger brand took over, which was committed to using Icelandic meat. Even alcohol consumption fell significantly, defying predictions, but one as yet unverified theory has it that many Icelanders have begun making wine at home from fruit juices and yeast with some even distilling their own moonshine. Almost every week the police seized crops of cannabis grown in illicit greenhouses under artificial light, their producers given away by inflated electricity bills incurred during long, dark winters.

Yet not everything was negative in immediate post-crash Iceland, and the depreciation of the *króna* even created new opportunities for some. Tourism increased as prices dropped, while in the shipping sector there was a sharp increase in maintenance and repairs carried out locally. Critically ill Greenlanders now found themselves flown to Iceland rather than Denmark, nearer and suddenly half as expensive. Consumption, moreover, did not decline as steeply as had been feared, and the government allowed those most at risk of personal bankruptcy access to state pension funds in what became a stampede by the most financially disoriented sector of the population. It is hard to imagine how poor future generations of pensioners will be when they have to live on a meagre basic allowance.

Icelanders had taken out loans indexed on foreign currencies, and their debts doubled almost as soon as the *króna* collapsed in value. It was also imperative to stop property prices from collapsing, and so Icelanders had their heads held above water while they carried on paying their debts.

The slow-down in domestic consumption was real enough but it had little impact on employment as almost all consumer goods are imported. A country that has always had a negative trade balance was for once spectacularly in the black. Some businesses' debts were wiped clean to prevent them from going under. Iceland's stock exchange, which had lost 97 per cent of its share value, was running on empty. Fifteen strategic enterprises appeared on a secret list to be helped through insolvency. Among those that would have faced bankruptcy if they had not been helped by the state-backed banks were Icelandair and Iceland Express (airlines), Eimskip (shipping), Sjóvá and VÍS (insurance), Penninn-Eymundsson (bookshops) and *Morgunblaðið* (newspaper). In short, except from fishing companies and those businesses that quit Iceland voluntarily or not (Össur, Actavis), the country's private sector looked as bleak as the high plains of its interior.

Iceland applied to join the European Union in July 2009. The move was met with general indifference on the island where seventy per cent of people are against EU membership but mostly wish negotiations to be fully explored.

Portraits of Poverty

Signs of extreme poverty and suffering are not easy to spot on the streets of Reykjavik. The homeless do not sleep on the streets, in summer or winter, and there are hostels for men, for women and by the harbour for couples. Nor is hardship detectable among those who are about to lose their apartments because their mortgages, based on foreign currency values, have doubled while their income has remained the same. The banks have been ordered by the government to turn these bankrupt homeowners into tenants in their own properties. Children can thus stay in their local schools and the move averts a sense of panic about property prices that would drive prices even lower. And yet the crisis is very much here in the stock market, in abandoned projects and all the time in everybody's mind.

Heimir Magnússon, married with three children, is in the process of losing his house. He was born 49 years ago in an isolated fjord district in the north-east, Vopnafjörður, which sees a brief Indian summer at the beginning of autumn each year. He worked on a trawler after studying mechanics and then gave up fishing to raise mink and silver foxes, highly strong animals that do not thrive near an airport or a busy road. The market for furs was buoyant and many Icelanders, perhaps too many, became involved, but after a year Heimir realized that he needed proper training, which he acquired in Finland. After fifteen years, however, he went bust due to too much competition and general hostility to the fur trade. Following his brother's example he then qualified as a pilot, after intensive training that was financed through a bank loan, and brought his family to live in Reykjavik, having found work first in Scotland then as the pilot of a private jet owned by one of the New Vikings of international capitalism. The 2008 crash brought the company in question to its knees, Heimir was fired and he found work for a few months as a builder in order to pay the bills. A friend then mentioned a gold mine in Greenland where a mechanic was needed, and he found himself returning to his first line of work repairing the machinery used for dynamiting rock faces. At the mine there was neither a village nor road, just a few huts, a landing stage and a helicopter to take the workers to the nearest airfield. The mine itself had come into being thanks to climate change, gold prospectors unlike polar bears benefitting from receding snow and ice. But the company Heimir was working for was Icelandic and on 31 December 2009 it made its entire workforce redundant, offering to rehire them with a fifteen per cent cut in salary. It was an offer difficult to refuse, even if Heimir knew then that he would not be able to save his house.

Unlike the fishing areas that witnessed an unexpected boom due to a doubling of prices, the capital and its suburbs sank into a brooding decline. In an economic landscape where only eleven per cent of businesses could survive without the artificial intervention of the nationalized banks everybody had to adapt to a new reality. There were even ironic role reversals, where the bankrupt former rich looked like the real losers, while those who had nothing already before the crisis found that little had changed and even seemed rather cheerful in the wintry mood of depression.

Some were worried by rising unemployment while others were concerned about what would happen when the £3 billion debt accrued by the online bank Icesave had to be paid back to British and Dutch investors who saw their savings disappear. Despite months of parliamentary wrangling and media debate Icelanders admitted that they failed to understand the issue.

The hero of the "kitchenware revolution" was the singer Hörður Torfason, who turned his trailer into an improvised stage and with his simple slogans was the catalyst or support act that warmed up the crowds in Reykjavik before giving way to the bigger political names. Since then he has done nothing to take advantage of his celebrity status. Thirty years previously he had set up an organization for Icelandic gays then had had to seek exile for several years after receiving death threats. There is nothing anarchistic about what he says on the question of debt: "we're guilty of gambling with other people's money, and we have to pay it back. When will we grow up and accept that everything has to be paid for, and that we can't always find excuses for what only we think is a special case?"

Anglo-Icelandic Tensions

Bad news began to emerge from Britain (and Denmark, see below) in the spring of 2008. In an article in *The Daily Telegraph* Iceland was likened to "one big toxic hedge fund". "The story doesn't make sense any more," the paper continued, "nobody wants anything to do with it." Two days later *The Times* remarked that Iceland's financial reputation was already damaged and was in danger of becoming a self-fulfilling prophecy: "The uncomfortable fact for Iceland is that the rumours and talk of a crisis could create the crisis." In Iceland, meanwhile, there was no sense of panic and only a handful of insiders discreetly withdrew their deposits from the banks. The gloomy prognostications of the British press were noticed, but largely dismissed as another instance of ill-will on the part of the old adversary.

Then the country's second biggest bank, the now nationalized Landsbankinn, found it was unable to refinance itself. It founded an online subsidiary Icesave, which offered its prospective customers seven per cent interest on their savings, paid monthly, and a guarantee from the Icelandic state that was made without the government's knowledge but, unfortunately for Iceland, real enough. What happened to the funds collected from some 200,000 British individuals and institutions in Britain and 120,000 in the Netherlands? Part of the money, frozen in Britain, has been used to reimburse customers up to a limit of €20,000 each, while another part—although this has not been confirmed—was used to finance the sumptuous Harpa concert hall. The rest disappeared into thin air in the months before the crash.

Icesave's collapse, along with that of its mother company, created a sense of the absurd in Iceland; there was no problem, it was argued, as the missing money was to be repaid in distant Britain. Furthermore, popular anger and frustration focused on the Icesave issue, perhaps because it was easier to blame a foreign enemy than to look closer to home.

A pressure group was formed, InDefence, which circulated a petition signed by about 70,000 people. The Icelandic president, who had been involved with the financiers responsible for the country's downfall, saw the opportunity to rebuild his popularity with a cunning populist manoeuvre and submitted the repayment agreement to a referendum, which duly rejected it. Parliament, with left and right working together, then submitted a second agreement, this time more weighted in favour of Iceland after several British and Dutch concessions, which the president again refused to ratify. A new referendum produced the same result, and the whole affair was sent to be considered by the European Union's Court of Justice and the European Free Trade Area's Surveillance Authority.

When the British authorities resorted to anti-terrorist legislation to freeze Icelandic assets, Icelanders were stunned but hardly reacted, so great was the malaise caused by the collapse. Only later, when the campaign to resist repaying the Icesave debt was organized, was the issue added to a briefly virulent outbreak of anti-British feeling. The centre-right opposition saw in Icesave a heaven-sent pretext to attack the government for being overly conciliatory with the British. Calm was restored when it transpired that the assets frozen in Britain would enable the debt to be repaid.

Boom and Bust in Britain and Denmark

This, according to *On Thin Ice* by Jón F. Thoroddsen, is a partial list of what a few Icelanders came to own in Britain:

The Baugur Group (Jón Ásgeir Jóhannesson and his father Jóhannes Jónsson): House of Fraser, Karen Millen, Hamleys, Whittard of Chelsea, Goldsmiths, Iceland (35%), Royal Unibrew (26%), Refresco (48%), Bayrock Group LLC (50%), French Connection (7.8%), Woolworths group (4.7%), Debenhams (13.5%), Moss Bros. (28.5%).

Björgólfur Guðmundsson and his son Björgólfur Thor Björgólfsson: West Ham United FC, Icesave, Heritable Bank, Teather & Greenwood, Stockbrokers.

The Bakkavör Group, owned by brothers Lýður and Ágúst Guðmundsson, became in 2008 the UK's biggest manufacturer of prepared food after its takeover of ready meals supplier Geest. It produced over 6,000 products in 18 categories, which were developed and sold predominantly under its customers' own brand names.

The oligarchs' megalomania in Britain drew them towards all that glistered: banking, fashion and gold (the Goldsmiths jewellery chain), while the more traditional import-export magnates or their representatives continued in the fish processing business. The shopping spree sometimes took infantile forms such as when the young Jón Ásgeir Jóhannesson—reportedly worth more than £600 million—bought Hamleys and proudly had the firm's logo displayed on a Formula 1 car that he brought into Iceland and put on show in a Reykjavik shopping centre that he owned.

In Denmark the Icelandic feeding frenzy reflected an inferiority complex in relation to the Danes and a desire to avenge the bad marks received in primary school Danish examinations. One oligarch bought the Hotel d'Angleterre, the best hotel in Copenhagen, and it was said that in the bidding process his offer was twice that of his nearest competitor. The same Jón Ásgeir acquired Magasin du Nord, the most prestigious of Danish department stores, but he also dreamed of dominating the Danish press and created through his Baugur Group a free daily paper, *Nyhedsavisen*, which was distributed every morning to half a million homes. The formula had worked in Iceland whose unfortunate inhabitants had hitherto been forced to choose between a good investigative newspaper that also specialised in gossip to maintain its readership and a right-wing daily supported by the wealthy elite as a means of defending their interests. Fortunately perhaps, *Nyhedsavisen* collapsed in 2008, but not before it had earned the enmity of Danish journalists. Even before its problems in Britain, Iceland—or rather its oligarchs—had lost its innocence in Denmark.

In early 2013 Jón Ásgeir Jóhannesson complained that allegations of improper links between his Baugur Group and the failed Glitnir bank amounted to politically motivated persecution. In *Fréttablaðið* the London-based magnate remarked: "I am saddened that I have been persecuted by the authorities for 10 years. From August 2002 I have been an official suspect [in criminal inquiries]. This has been a heavy burden for me and my family ... That is what is happening in this case and others."

Old and New

A centre-right coalition emerged victorious from the elections of April 2013, and the real winner was the Progressive Party, whose leader Sigmundur Davið Gunnlaugsson was invited by the president to form a new government. The conservative Independence Party, with its second worst result ever, was still suffering from its perceived role in the 2008 crash. Two new political groupings born from divisions within the left—the Pirate Party and Bright Future—won seats, their names reflecting scepticism among large sectors of the population with the established parties and their promises.

The new government intends to reduce imports by increasing domestic production and by expanding the hydroelectric and geothermal energy sectors. The environmental precautions initiated by the preceding government are to be sidelined, as is suggested by the new rulers's first symbolic act: the post of minister of the environment was abolished.

5

The Written Word
The City in Literature

Language of the Vikings

It is impossible to talk about Icelandic literature without mentioning the language in which it is written. Icelandic is more or less the language spoken by the Vikings a thousand years ago and it is little changed because of Iceland's historical isolation and small population, unlike in other Scandinavian countries. Icelandic is, as a result, an archaic language with a plethora of declensions and conjugations that can be a real headache for the foreigner. The definite article comes after the noun, meaning that both must be declined, while adjectives are strong or weak and masculine, feminine and neuter each have their own declension. The subjunctive has survived in the present tense and in all past tenses. There are four cases: nominative, accusative, dative and genitive, and in pronunciation the stress is invariably on the first syllable. Icelanders are very proud of their language, insisting that their children speak it correctly.

Icelandic is a beautiful language, very rich and homogenous, and the concepts it expresses, as in German, often take the form of compound nouns whose meaning is immediately accessible to native speakers as the linguistic roots are neither Greek nor Latin but originally Icelandic. It is not an idiomatic language but one that demands considerable respect for its grammatical rules. It is also nowadays a language of farmers and peasants largely used by city dwellers, with innumerable expressions related to agriculture and spoken in a rather monotone fashion, in a way that is intended to conceal feelings and emotions. Within several generations its intonations will no doubt be transformed and it will become an even more beautiful language, unchanged in essence if not in tone because its declensions protect and conserve it. Icelanders, it seems, cannot use a foreign word without declining it.

Medieval manuscript (courtesy Visit Reykjavik)

Written in the twelfth century, the sagas tell of events that happened in the ninth and tenth centuries when Reykjavik was a *vík*, an isolated bay with a scattering of settlements. Yet despite their historical distance it is impossible to underestimate the importance of these tales for an entire people as a record of their origins. In order to get a sense of current research into the age of colonization, it is worth visiting the 871+/-2 Museum, situated in the basement of the beautiful Hotel Centrum, itself built around one of the capital's oldest houses. Here we see that concern for historical accuracy and intellectual honesty have become so important among the country's historians that what was meant at first to be a museum in honour to the first colonist, Ingólfur Arnarson, has become a much more modest collection that allows itself a few conjectures about the small piles of stones found on this spot. While these historians try to demystify and separate sagas from historical truth, the tourist industry continues to sell the Viking brand at every opportunity. Even the Viking waxworks in the Saga Museum, housed in the spectacular Perlan (Pearl) installation, can be something of an anticlimax, especially for those who have visited York's Jorvik Centre.

There is no escaping the evidence or lack of it, and so understanding the sagas lies in the sagas themselves. The best approach is perhaps to read one of them in its entirety rather than fragments or to visit the places where they are thought to have taken place. The most famous of the works are the *Laxdæla saga*, the *Grettis saga*, *Njáls saga* and *Egil's saga* or the saga of Egill Skallagrímsson. For anyone wishing to make a journey from Reykjavik in search of any of these, the dark *Grettis saga*, with its emphasis on exile, is the least suitable since the spectacular Skagafjörður fjord is far away and it is impossible to reach the outcrop of Drangey Island most of the year—although Grettir allegedly swam there. It is tempting to follow in the footsteps of the *Njáls saga* and see the volcanoes of Hekla (generally lost in the clouds) and the infamous and unpronounceable Eyjafjallajökull, but here the sites are far apart, while the places associated with the *Laxdæla saga*, in the west of the country, are also remote. *Egil's saga* is therefore a good choice as Borgarnes (Digranes in the saga) is more or less an hour away by car via the Hvalfjörður fjord tunnel. At Borgarnes itself, at the place where Egill's father is said to have pursued and killed a female servant, are two small museums, a restaurant, and quite often Kjartan Ragnarsson, the museums' creator and a successful producer at the National Theatre who suddenly decided to move here. Headphones allow visitors to follow the exhibitions in various languages, one museum dealing with colonization, the other with the saga itself. The best course of action is to start with a visit to the museum devoted to *Egil's saga* followed by a tour of the saga's sites.

Egil's saga: Monster, Poet and Hero

The King of Norway, Haraldur, swore that he would not cut his hair until he had definitively established his authority. One of the chieftains who suffered from the monarch's consolidation of power was Kveldúlfur (evening wolf), Egill Skallagrímsson's grandfather, who owed his name to the fact that he was tired and irritable in the evening. He was also believed to possess supernatural powers. Haraldur killed the son of Kveldúlfur whose revenge in turn was pitiless as, assisted by Egill, he murdered two of Haraldur's cousins and more than fifty of their men. The two outlaws seized a boat and set sail for Iceland with women and children, their lives in danger in Norway. Egill's father died during the journey but Egill settled at a place called Borg near today's Borgarnes, where nearby were forests, salmon rivers and seals. Fish abounded in the sea and swans and all types of birds were to be found in the area.

But Egill could not stay quietly out of trouble. He set off again for Norway, ruled by Haraldur's son Eiríkur Blóðöx (Eric Bloodaxe) and Queen Gunnhildur, said to practise magic. At a feast where Egill drank more than he should have the queen attempted to poison him but he noticed the ruse, threw his drinking horn away and killed as an accomplice one of his host's sons. Forced to flee, he made it to England, where he became chieftain of *Jórvík* (York) and eventually an adversary of King Athelstan the Victorious. He was captured and was to be killed the following day but composed during the night a splendid poem that earned him the king's mercy. Back in Iceland, Egill settled once more at Mosfell near Reykjavik where he died. Here, according to the saga, are two chests full of silver given to him by King Athelstan.

Egill's education aimed to make a Viking of him, a man who one day would take his chance on the sea. As a child he wrote this poem:

> My mother said
> A boat will be bought
> A boat and five oars,
> To sail with the Vikings
> Command the precious craft
> And then reach the harbour
> And kill a man and another

He had an older brother, Thorolf, of whom he was jealous—a jealousy that he inherited from his father. At the age of twelve he was playing one winter evening with his father and a boy eight years older than him, Thord, and the two youths got the better of the older man. But later Skallagrim, Egill's father, gathered his strength, seized Thord, threw him to ground and killed him on the spot. Then he set about attacking Egill. But Skallagrim had a servant woman named Thorgerd Brak, who had formed Egill when he was a child. She was an imposing woman, as strong as a man and well versed in the Magic Arts. Brak said, "you are attacking your son like a man beast, Skallagrim." Skallagrim let Egill go, but went for her instead. She fled, with Skallagrim in pursuit. They came to the shore at the end of Digranes, and she ran off the edge of the cliff and swam away. Skallagrim threw a huge boulder after her which struck her between the shoulder blades. Neither the woman nor the boulder ever came up afterwards. That spot is now called Brákarsund (Brak's Channel). Egill was furious, refusing to join the others at a meal:

> Then he walked into the room and went over to Skallagrim's favour-
> ite, a man who was in charge of the workers and ran the farm with
> him. Egill killed him with a single blow, then went to his seat.
> Skallagrim did not mention the matter and it was let rest afterwards,
> but father and son did not speak to each other, neither kind nor
> unkind words, and so it remained through the winter.

Brákarsund lies near to the museum devoted to *Egil's saga* at Borgarnes, where the store-house has been converted into a theatre that in 2011 hosted a play where Brak is the central character. The six lines of the saga in which she appears have been transformed into a play, rather like the way in which Mary Magdalene has inspired a rich literary tradition despite her brief appearance in the New Testament.

The adult Egill and his brother Thorolf entered the service of Athelstan, King of England. The unknown author of the saga estimates that Scotland accounted for a third of the Britain at the time and Northumbria a fifth.

Olaf the Red was the King of Dublin and managed to seize Northumbria, leading to battle with Athelstan. The build-up to war is described in great detail, with messengers carrying peace proposals between the rival camps, Athelstan demanding that Olaf retreat and his enemy refusing. (It should be pointed out that *Egil's saga* cannot be read as a direct account of the famous 937 Battle of Brunanburth, as Egill could not have taken place—despite the Icelandic tendency to read sagas as history.)

Egill led a troop of men, his brother Thorolf following with a standard. But when Thorolf was killed Egill fought with such fury that his enemies fled. "Egill and his men pursued them, killing everyone they could catch, and it was pointless for anyone to ask for his life to be spared." Here is the trademark concision of the Icelandic saga; little is said, and there is no need to add anything more.

King Athelstan showered Egill with gifts and gave him two chests to present to his father. "These chests are yours, Egill. And if you go to Iceland, you will present this money to your father, which I am sending him as compensation for the death of his son." The king wanted Egill to remain in England, but Egill refused. "When spring came, Egill announced to the King that he intended to leave for Norway that summer and find out about the situation of Asgerd, who was his brother Thorolf's wife. "They have amassed plenty of wealth", said Egill, "but I do not know whether any of their children are still alive. I must provide for them if they are alive, but shall inherit everything if Thorolf has died childless."

In his later years Egill came to live at Mosfell, now a suburb of Reykjavik. At the end of the saga those around him have converted to Christianity but Egill, now blind, wishes to die as he has lived:

> One evening when everyone was going to bed at Mosfell, Egill called in two of Grim's slaves.
>
> He told them to fetch him a horse, "because I want to bathe in the pool".
>
> When he was ready he went out, taking his chests of silver with him. He mounted the horse, crossed the hayfields to the slope that begins there and disappeared.
>
> In the morning, when all the people got up, they saw Egill wandering around the hill, east of the farm, leading a horse behind him. They went over to him and brought him home.
>
> But neither the slaves nor the chests of the treasure ever returned, and there are many theories about where Egill hid his treasure.

Here we are closer to *Treasure Island* than to Icelandic sagas, which normally leave little space for elements of mystery. The saga's author (Snorri Sturluson, according to many including Torfi Tulinius) offers various hypotheses as to where the treasure was buried. It has never been found, unsurprisingly, since this is a work of fiction. Yet here already can be seen the Icelandic hero *par excellence*, who travels abroad to cover himself in glory, whether by force of arms or poetic inspiration, and who returns to his native Iceland to end his days in relative obscurity. Whether or not Egill actually existed, the myth was forged and it was to produce many imitators. The New Vikings, who before 2008 tried to buy parts of Denmark and Britain, were the direct descendants of Egill—with less brutality but perhaps more cunning.

Literary Visitors

Sabine Baring-Gould was born in Exeter in 1834 and died just before his ninetieth birthday in the parish of Lewtrenchard in West Devon, of which he had been the parson, squire and justice of the peace. His travel book *Iceland: Its Scenes and Sagas* was published in 1863 and he also wrote two novels with Icelandic themes, *Grettir the Outlaw* and *The Icelander's Sword*. The vicar-writer led an eccentric life with a chaotic education and upbringing, and he married a woman half his age whom he first sent for three years to finishing school in York to learn "middle-class manners"—she would eventually have fifteen children with him.

Baring-Gould could be devastating in his observations and his sense of superiority could easily pass for arrogance if he did not always take care to mock himself. His book on Iceland is nonetheless a mine of information on the contemporary society, the flora and fauna and the country's geology. Reykjavik appears in the second chapter like some poverty-stricken metropolis from the developing world where the tourist struggles to shake off a crowd of hangers-on:

The town is full of idle men, who follow the stranger whithersoever he goes—provided he does not walk too fast for them. They hang about the stores as thickly and stupidly as flies round a sugar barrel. They stream into the shops after me, throng so closely round me that I can hardly move, listen to what I say, eye me from head to foot, ask the price of every article of clothing I have on, . . . criticize my purchases, want to examine my purse, but I object, and by so doing, hurt the feeling of half a dozen.

They make advances towards familiarity, shaking my hands, asking my name, then my father's name, then they inquire who was my mother; they offer me a pinch of snuff, or rather a pull at their snuff-horns, which are like powder-flasks, and are applied to the nostril, the head thrown back, and the snuff poured in, till the nose is pretty well choked. One man, very dirty and very drunk, insists of having a kiss—the national salutation; and when the merchant explains that such is not the English custom, he kisses all the natives in the shop, and embraces the merchant across the counter.

A travelling companion from the United States, Mr. Briggs, is disappointed that the country is not more exotic. He complains to Baring-Gould:

> "There is not the slightest use in coming to Iceland!"
>
> "How so?"
>
> "Why, it is just like everywhere else! I have been looking in at one of the stores, and what do you think I saw? Crinolines, real crinolines, man! Hanging up for sale. Crinolines! Is it not horrible? We are not beyond the range of fashion yet!"

(Fashion was indeed spreading fast through nineteenth-century Reykjavik. A ball was organized in the capital in 1861 in honour of the visit of Napoleon III's cousin, and the prince's entourage had asked the invited Icelandic ladies to attend in national costume— they all arrived in Danish-made evening dresses inspired by French fashion designs.)

Before leaving Reykjavik Baring-Gould called on the Catholic priest, seeking reassurance that the country he has visited is worthy of the interest he has shown in it.

> "I suppose," said I, "that the country and the scenery are most magnificent."
>
> "Magnificent indeed," answered the abbé; "there is the magnificence of Satan imprinted deep in the face of this land. Did you ever hear the Danish account of the origin of Iceland?"
>
> "Never," I replied.
>
> "Well, then; after the creation, Satan was rather taken aback, and he thought within himself, 'I'll see now what I can do!' So he toiled at creation, and lo! He turned out Iceland. This myth gives you a notion of the place: all is horrible and gloomy."

Like W. H. Auden, William Morris made two trips to Iceland, but with only two years separating them the second was more a deepening of his experience than an opportunity to notice differences. Morris is the only one of these writers to have used his visit as a personal escape, a break in a difficult time of his life. He was 37 when he arrived in Iceland, was married to the artist's model Jane Burden, who was also the mistress of his friend the painter Dante Gabriel Rossetti. Kelmscott Manor in Oxfordshire was the scene of a *ménage-à-trois*, but Morris was to remain married to Jane until his death. A woman and two men form the subject of the *Laxdæla Saga* which Morris translated but never published and to which he devoted a long poem.

But Morris' diary remains mysterious, and it is unclear how he reconciled Iceland's harsh reality with his own private aesthetic and his growing socialist convictions. He admired the country, its landscapes and light but generally through a prism of greyness—the adjective "grey" appears more than a hundred times in his diary, applied in turn to lava, moss, rivers, clouds, cliffs, plains, sky, sea and hills. We are far from the exuberant vegetation, the strawberries and daisies of his wallpaper designs. We may wonder what aesthetic emotions he was looking for in this bare and hostile land.

The Icelanders whom he met on his travels were of a different sort from the heroic characters of the sagas, but Morris was the only one of the literary travellers to treat them with respect notwithstanding his frequent irritation. A year later Richard Burton, better known for his explorations in Africa, described Reykjavik in unflattering terms: "the Icelandic capital, with its tumble down wooden houses, its foul drains and ancient and fish-like smells is not likely to be an object of admiration to any traveller." Morris, on the other hand, observed more judiciously in his diary: "A little after dinner we go ashore and land in a street of little low wooden houses, pitched, and with white sash frames; the streets of black volcanic sand; little ragged gardens about some of the houses growing potatoes, cabbages and huge stems of angelica: not a very attractive place, yet not very bad, better than a north-country town in England." This was not diplomacy on Morris' part, as the diary was never intended for publication, but it was the same attitude that brought him to conclude that "the most grinding poverty is a trifling evil compared with the inequality of classes." His view of Iceland, or more particularly of the early years of its colonization, was the romantic one that prevailed at the time, and to this extent Morris could not transcend a cliché:

> Iceland's first settlers were of the best families of Norway, men of bold and independent spirit, who could not brook what they deemed the oppression of the early form of feudality forced upon the free men of the tribes at the time when Harold Hairfair was winning his way to the sole sovereignty of Norway . . . The race of which these warlike exiles formed an especially noble part had an inborn genius for poetry and the dramatic expression of events doubtless quickened amongst the settlers in Iceland by the energy which the struggle for life in a rough climate and barren land forced upon the brave and generous, if somewhat masterful men.

This idealized version of the first Icelandic colonists overlooks the fact that in the tenth century some 2,000 free men ruled harshly over 50,000 landless serfs and slaves.

W. H. Auden spent a few months in Iceland in 1936 and then returned in 1965. He felt that that country had changed rapidly in the interval between his two trips and hankered after his first experience while recognizing that Icelanders wanted to modernize: "For the visitor, there is one loss. As I flew up to the North-West to stay for three days at a farm where I had stayed in 1936, I pictured to myself the pleasure of riding in the afternoons. But the farmer had exchanged his ponies for a Land-Rover. Sensible of him, but disappointing for me."

At the time of Auden's second visit Jean-Paul Sartre and Simone de Beauvoir were spending a few days in Reykjavik. While Sartre got drunk in his room in the Hotel Borg, de Beauvoir travelled to the north of the island with the celebrated explorer Paul Emile Victor. She recalled in her autobiography her surprise at Icelandic farmers travelling by airplane and was astonished to see inveterate alcoholics, when they had nothing to drink, eating shoe polish.

The Hotel Borg was for many years the only good hotel in Reykjavik and the place where all Icelandic singers and performers appeared. It was completed in 1930 and it was there that British officers would go to drink beer while the local population was forbidden to do so. The restaurant and ballroom have kept something of their Art Deco charm but have also suffered from clumsy attempts at updating. Situated opposite the parliament building, the hotel has changed hands several times in recent years without ever rediscovering its previous allure.

Halldór Laxness

Winner of the Nobel Prize for Literature in 1955, Halldór Kiljan Laxness (1902-88) was during his lifetime the undisputed giant of Icelandic letters. Several biographies published since his death have slightly tarnished the image of the great man but he remains a figure who, without sentimentality, has inspired generations of Icelanders. Reykjavik, where he was born but left as a young child, occupies a relatively modest place in his work and appears principally in two works. In the 1957 *Brekkukotsannáll* (*The Fish Can Sing*) we follow the lives of a poor family and their rich counterpart, whose prodigal son dreams of becoming a famous singer in Denmark—a dream that will be illusory. Reykjavik appears as hardly urban, more like a big village:

> I was walking down Long Street, as the main street in Reyjavik used to be called in those days, where Gudmundsen's store and the theological seminary and the Hotel d'Islande stood. It was just after midday. The weather was dry. I was watching a train of pack-ponies loaded with stockfish moving off; in those days farmers bought dried cod's heads and transported them on ponies out of the eastern districts on journeys as log, measured in days as a journey from Paris to Peking, through countless districts, over mountains and moors and across rocky deserts and rushing rivers; it was a most impressive sight to see such a train setting off; there was about it an atmosphere of distant eastern places.

Atómstöðin (*The Atomic Station*) also takes place in Reykjavik in the aftermath of the Second World War. Here again two social milieus are contrasted in the form of a wealthy middle-class family and a young female servant, Ugla, who works for them. Ugla decides finally to return to the village of Sauðárkrókur, a decision heavy in implications for Icelandic literature as Reykjavik would have to wait many years before attracting the attention of the country's novelists.

Modern Icelandic Poetry

In any Icelandic family home rows of books occupy pride of place, in the sitting room preferably and never hidden away in a corridor. These books are usually nicely bound and among them are almost inevitably volumes of poetry. Poetry may have lost some of its importance among younger generations who prefer to express themselves through music, but the genre is very much alive. Traditional, even archaic, forms survive, especially in the countryside; epic rhyming *rímur* are chanted, almost sung, while four-verse *vísur* generally contain a comic element and satirize current events.

Icelanders love political meetings where poetry readings alternate with speeches. Obituaries often end with a well-known poem, which may have no obvious connection with the deceased. When public figures such as priests, parliamentarians or judges are found in compromising situations, *vísur* immediately proliferate, often suggestive and salacious but also obeying very strict rules of versification.

The patience shown by Icelanders in poetry reading evenings, when young poets rarely know when to stop, is astonishing, and it must be admitted that poetry is often badly read in Iceland, declaimed without the slightest hint of emotion even though those listening, touched by the skill or profundity of the poet, are moved within themselves. With the stress invariably on the first syllable, the beginning of each line seems heavily ponderous, while the intonation can sound highly monotonous. Icelandic poetry, rich and evocative, deserves to be read alone for the reader's personal pleasure. Several twentieth-century poets have contributed to a significant modern tradition (the extracts below are translated by Sigurður A. Magnússon).

Snorri Hjartarson (1906-86) was a painter before devoting himself to poetry and until 1981 was head of Reykjavik's municipal library. For him Iceland's bare, treeless and empty landscape was not a subject for dainty versifying. His verse evokes the sky, sea, wind, the occasional bird—using an infinity of words in Icelandic to describe them, the richness of vocabulary compensating for the limitations of the subject matter.

Journey (extract)
Each road from home
is a road leading home.

The wheel of day turns fast,
the castle by the spring
and the camp ground by the river
are lost far behind,
dusk falls and the moon's sickle
is lifted against the stars.
. . .
The night will be long
chilly and dark.

But beyond the mountains,
beyond the cardinal points and the night
the tower of light rises
where time sleeps.

Into time's peace and dream
the journey is planned.

Steinn Steinarr (1908-58) is a unanimously loved and respected poet in Iceland and a precursor in his use of free verse. His inspiration, radical and socially conscious in the inter-war years, gradually evolved into lyricism that was close to abstraction where the magic of words and rhymes triumphed. A self-taught writer without being, in the Scandinavian sense of the term, a proletarian poet, Steinn Steinarr was one of the first Icelandic authors to make a living from his work. A medical condition affecting his arm, which made him unable to do any manual work, determined his vocation.

Time and Water (extract)

1

Time is like the water,
and the water is deep and cold
as my own awareness.
And time is like an unfinished portrait
painted jointly
by the water and me.

And time and the water
run out aimlessly
Into my awareness.
. . .

3

On translucent wings
the water flies back
against its own
resistance.

The tangerine clue,
running on before me,
follows no direction.

Beyond the bloodthirsty lips
of burning matter
the flower of death is growing.

On a foursquare plane
between circle and cone
the white flower of death is growing.

Jón úr Vör (1917-2000) enjoyed celebrity in his homeland for his collection, *The Village* (1946), but he was never again able to recapture this volume's felicity of expression. The universe evoked was that of cod drying in the sun, the fish factory, the village that the bare mountain seemed to push into the sea, and men at work. The fish factory that he took as his model is still there in the village of

Patreksfjörður, but society has changed with such speed that fiction is arguably better than poetry at capturing such a transformation.

Lean Months (extract)
And do you remember the long
   milkless midwinter days,
   the lean months' fry,
   salted chips soaked in a pail,
   the well house
     and the plain song of a running water,
   boats in their cribs
     covered with canvas,
   sheep on the shore,
     and cold feet,
  and evenings long as eternity,
often then impatiently waiting
for fishing weather
and fresh catch for the pot.

And do you remember
  one evening at dusk.
  You stood on the beach with your foster mother.
  Staring in fear at frozen rollers,
  out over the fjord,
  into the sky -
  you expected a small boat to round the headland,
  but it did not come.
  And dusk turned to heavy darkness with a roaring storm,
  silence
  and tears on a pillow,
  and you fell asleep alone in a bed too large.

And do you remember
  your joy in the middle of night,
  when you woke feeling on your head
  the touch of a calloused palm

and across your cheek
the soft warm stroke of the back of a hand.
Your foster father had returned
- and kissed you as you put your arms around his neck.

Stefán Hörður Grímsson (1920-2002) was a sailor in distant
countries and a swimming teacher in Iceland, a man of many pro-
fessions is a well established Icelandic tradition. A writer whose
work is rare and all the more valuable for it, he published only six
slim booklets, where verbal alchemy transfigures a reality that can
never be fully grasped. Modest, secretive and yet less retiring than
he seemed, Stefán Hörður Grímsson was the antithesis of the fashionable literary figure.

Winter Day (extract)
From the land's frigid face
the extinct eyes of lakes stare
at a gray February sky.

Of the wanderings of the restless winds
across the spacious vault
no news has been brought.
. . .
Under the hollow shell of silence
solitary bass tones keep reaching out
When the ice heart beats.

On their spindly legs
men cross the snowfields
with mountains on their shoulders.

Sigfús Daðason (1928-96) spent several years in France in the
1950s and was among the generation known as the "Atom Poets".
On his return he edited an important literary review, *Tímarit Máls
og Menningar*. The author of a mere four volumes, his approach,
sometimes esoteric in appearance, demands of the reader a deep
understanding of the nuances of Icelandic.

Pop Melody

The dream is as moonlight
the moonlight as a dream
as moonlight
the dream I finally had last night

as the sea as the moon as the wake
as eyes deep in the sea
as you forget me
as you recall me tonight
as sailing across the sea lonely and gray
as you come to me
as you come at last this night
as the wake in the moonlight
as the moon in the wake and the sea wide and lonely

Þorsteinn frá Hamri (1938-) is the last poet to have chosen as pseudonym—an ancient Icelandic tradition—the name of the farm where he was born (frá Hamri). The author of three novels and many translations, he is best-known for the fifteen collections of poetry that are rich in allusions to Scandinavian mythology and history. As with Sigfús Daðason, the reader is challenged in terms of attention to detail and language, and his poetry can be difficult even for Icelanders themselves.

Some Days

Some days are houses
which we lock with care
before leaving
to enter upon the stage of the years

but if we later pass them by
accidentally
we see all the doors open
and children playing in peace
and what is more important:
the sun shines with incredible brightness on the house.

Vilborg Dagbjartsdóttir (1930-) is a unique figure in Reykjavik's literary life. A teacher and feminist activist who is proud of her very modest origins, she has also written a great deal for children. She is the widow of the writer and poet Þorgeir Þorgeirson.

Missa Candelarium (extract)

III
Blessed be the small fingers
of my mother
who picked cotton grass in the marsh
Blessed be the rheumatic hands
of my grandmother
who wound the wick
Blessed be my grandfather
who fashioned a duck light out of iron
Blessed be my uncles
who melted down the cod liver oil
Blessed be the people
who endured the darkness
Blessed be the light
burning on a slender wick
a tiny flickering
in the polar night.

The Modern Novel

Icelandic literature long celebrated the virtues of the countryside as the place where wholesome lives were led and the language remained pure, while in Reykjavik it was tainted by Danish. The theme of Reykjavik as a city of sin has recently come back into vogue with contemporary crime fiction, much to the pleasure of local readers for whom criminality was hitherto restricted to distant and large metropolises. The countryside, meanwhile, is synonymous with boredom but conceals unspeakable secrets that are only revealed in the last pages.

Reykjavik, it has been said, grew too quickly from childhood to adulthood, bypassing adolescence. The novels of Ásta Sigurðardóttir (1930-72) deal with the 1940s and 1950s and tell the tales of young female *déracinées*, attracted by the foreign troops who were occupying the town. She writes of false hopes, anticipated disappointments and destitution with a moving sensibility. A young woman, pregnant and ill, who lives in a shanty dwelling built by the British military, is visited by her friend who tells her to go to a specialist, in other words to have an abortion. Both women have been in *ástandið* (literally, "the situation"), meaning that they have been sleeping with foreign troops, British then American.

"But you must go to see the specialist," said her friend. "You're crazy to do nothing. God, I don't know what I'd do without him, I'd be dead."

But you need to have someone to love," said the young sick woman hesitatingly. "Not from time to time, but all day, all night, someone to cherish, something beautiful, forever . . . That's how I want to live."

"Forever!" interrupted her friend. "What's left at the end of the day? Nothing at all. I thought I'd keep Djimm (Jim) forever, that we were in love. My God! A couple of nights and then goodbye, he was gone. You thought you could keep little Sissi even after Djonn (John) had disappeared! One year. And then she was dead from meningitis. You end up losing everything. And as for keeping these flowers in this slum, I ask you, it's not like you're living in a posh house!"

Pétur Gunnarsson (1947-) has colourfully evoked what life was like for a child and then a young adult at the beginning of the 1960s in an often extremely amusing trilogy. His books, which are now studied in schools, allow today's youth to understand what life was like for their parents.

Fathers disappear in the morning only to reappear around midday. They come back with their stubbly cheeks into the hushed world of mothers, with their prohibitions, their rules of hygiene and their imposed good manners and above all with their insistence that silence be observed when the radio is on.

After lunch fathers lie down with their jackets as pillows and with a broken matchstick in their mouth. And when the woman on the radio has finished telling them what the weather will be like, they get up and go back to work with a full thermos and some freshly buttered slices of bread.

And life becomes maternal and hushed again.

Mother in the laundry with a bundle of dirty washing.

Mother hanging the washing on the line with her mouth full of pegs.

Mother in the sitting room ironing and darning.

Mother in the kitchen cutting off the haddock's head.

Mother yawning on the bed as she mumbles sleepy stories.

In contrast, the more recent "swinging Reykjavik" has been very well captured by Hallgrímur Helgason in his novel *101 Reykjavik*, which was turned into a film. The book has enjoyed such success that 101, the postcode of those who live in the centre of Reykjavik, has become a sort of social status symbol. To be 101 is to be cool, part of the artistic elite or the bohemian middle class.

The Reykjavik of the 1990s had suddenly become modern, free, shorn of its complexes, a city where people were coming from the country or from abroad to enjoy themselves:

"It's two o'clock by the time I work myself through the darkness of the night down the side road. I'm going out to check out the night life. Get pissed and chase women. Nah. I follow the white stripe but occasionally grope through the bushes on the side of the road, searching for females. Didn't have the guts to take the car. Icelandic nightlife . . . Yes! I brought my old fellow walkman along for the trip: the only survival kit I have, apart from a brand new pack of extra strong country condoms, just in case."

According to Daisy L. Neijmann, much contemporary Icelandic fiction combines the modern with allusions to the ancient sagas, creating a sort of local magical realism:

> In recent Icelandic fiction, references to or elements from the sagas are incorporated as part of contemporary life in Reykjavik, together with the Beatles, rap, clubbing and grunge . . . Characters effortlessly spice up their English-based street-Icelandic with quotes from Sturla Þórðarson and Egill Skallagrímsson. The narratives delight in storytelling and storytellers, as leaps of wild and boundless imagination propel the characters forward, with a ghost lurking just around the next street corner. Iceland is full of ghosts. They are part of a traditional Icelandic perception of what constitutes reality, another important reason for the attraction of magical realism in Iceland.

Readers and Publishers

Eighty per cent of books in Iceland are sold at Christmas, when giving books to friends and relatives is a sort of moral duty. Icelanders acknowledge what they owe to their literature and are intent on preserving the tradition. Whether or not they read the books they buy or are given is a matter of conjecture. It is true that long winter nights encourage reading, and it has also been remarked that since 2008 the numbers using public libraries have risen significantly. Yet fewer people are to be seen reading a book on public transport or in a café than in many other countries.

Books are often beautifully bound, and beyond their contents they are considered objects of value and accorded a respect that is unknown elsewhere. A catalogue shared between publishers is distributed free of charge in every household, allowing readers to make their choices. Books are then exhibited every November and December on huge trestle tables in bookshops, where people come to browse, creating an atmosphere like in the celebrated communal hot baths—an opportunity for socializing. The first books published have the advantage of a clear field before the bestsellers appear, but the problem when the more eagerly awaited works arrive is that the lesser-known authors find their books relegated to the middle of the table where customers need long arms to reach them.

If the novels of established authors are generally preferred, there has also been a change in recent years with the vogue for crime fiction. Unknown in Icelandic literature until the last decade, the new *noir* novels now lead the bestsellers' list even after indifferent reviews.

Generally book sales are healthy, publishers less so and bookshops not at all. The Eymundsson bookshop chain, which dominates the local market, is regularly bailed out by its bank. Supermarkets start selling bestsellers before Christmas at spectacular discounts and books then disappear from their shelves while bookshops have to confront a dead season of ten months during which only twenty per cent of books are sold. Publishing remains a volatile business but printing has staged a comeback since 2008 and the collapse of the *króna* since it is no longer more expensive to print books in Iceland than abroad.

Reykjavik readers like autobiographies of living Icelanders. Some subjects such as the poet Vilborg Dagbjartsdóttir and Bryndís Schram, the wife of a politician, have inspired two autobiographies within a couple of years. But Icelandic autobiography is in fact biography, as although it may be written in the first person it is in fact the work of a ghost writer who collects, edits and re-writes the words of the supposed author. Even so, unlike bigger countries where anonymity is always a possibility, the name of the real author is always mentioned and nobody is led to believe that a show business or fashion celebrity can suddenly become a talented writer. Traditionally these biographies revealed little secrets or confirmed long-standing rumours, but nowadays private lives are already freely exposed in the press and as a result it has become harder to surprise or shock readers—which may explain a gradual decline in the life stories of the living.

Þorbjörg Pálsdóttir's *Dance* outside Perlan (Petr Kraumann)

6 | **Visual Images**
Art, Cinema and Drama

More than art itself, it is its social function that is most interesting in Iceland and its capital. Reykjavik's artistic heritage is meagre; its oldest houses date from the end of the eighteenth century, the Vikings left next to nothing, as did the centuries of poverty that followed. With the exception of a few tapestries and a handful of paintings, art is essentially a modern phenomenon.

The period of prosperity that followed the Second World War was beneficial for artists if not for art itself. It became a matter of status, almost an obligation, to show off shelves of bound books, and any self-respecting family also felt a duty to own some paintings. One of these, in particular, would have pride of place behind the sofa (a photograph exhibition was recently devoted to "sofa paintings", where furniture, wallpaper and the painting combined to create a scene of reassuring middle-class comfort). The "sofa painting" was generally large and traditionally showed a scene of countryside from which its owners originated. They were replaced by abstract artworks as the capital's links with the rural world weakened. But in almost all cases these canvases were genuine paintings and not reproductions or prints. Other pictures, often many of them, complemented the main "sofa painting" in the salon or sitting room without too much care devoted to the overall effect. And when space was at a premium the paintings were hung one on top of the other like in the wealthy European homes of the nineteenth century—which was also an age of prosperity. The post-war years were hence a happy time for painters since questions of price were generally secondary. The lack of an established heritage, a strongly democratic popular culture and the fact that few people had inherited paintings meant that all new artworks were sought after. The situation today is altogether different; there are many Icelanders who do not know what

to do with the heirlooms they have inherited, while auctions pitilessly reveal the real market value of artworks.

The visitor can get a good idea of Icelandic art through three
beautiful walks in Reykjavik. On a day when typically sun and
clouds, fine weather and showers, follow one after the other it makes
sense to head for the hill at Þingholt where by taking the lift (small
fee) one can admire the panorama from the viewing deck of the
Hallgrímskirkja. Guðjón Samúelsson, its architect, was also responsible for the National Theatre, the University's main building and
even the indoor swimming pool. Controversial but certainly original, the building was long compared to a giant phallus, but taller
towers have since taken from it its role as a landmark for fishing
boats in the bay. Nearby is the museum dedicated to the Symbolist
sculptor Einar Jónsson (1874-1954), where one can inspect the stat-
ues outside before deciding whether to view the interior. Some have
compared the museum to a sinister-looking mausoleum, but Einar
Jónsson's work has a monumental strength and spiritual complexity
that demand admiration.

Descending Skólavörðustígur, Reykjavik's artists' street, the
good and the less good rub shoulders. Here the visitor can get an
idea of the sorts of paintings that decorate Icelandic homes as well
as those that are aimed specifically at tourists and which reflect what
Icelanders take to be foreign tastes. Here too are some fine shops
selling beautiful jewellery and knitwear. Slowly coming down the
unpronounceable Skólavörðustígur, there are plenty of small galleries in the nearby streets and it is in one of these, Bergstaðastræti,
that stands the Ásgrímur Jónsson Museum, consecrated to Iceland's
first great artist and an innovator in the treatment of light and
perspective. As a pioneer Ásgrímur Jónsson (1876-1958) had the
responsibility of putting Iceland's landscapes on canvas for the first
time. In his greatest work, *Hekla* (1909) he depicts the majestic volcano rising from a grey-green foreground with a band of blue sky
above and then clouds. The composition is simple but it addresses
the main problem faced by any painter in Iceland—the representation of distance and the creation of perspective in a landscape where
no tree or house helps to measure distance. Ásgrímur's talent lay in

arranging foreground and background without artifice and in creating an astonishing sense of depth.

The small National Gallery of Iceland (Listasafn Íslands), close to Tjörnin, features permanent collections when a temporary exhibition is not on show, and it is interesting to see Icelandic landscapes interpreted through the prism of Impressionism, Cubism or Fauvism. Arguably a more original and personal vision can be appreciated at Kjarvalsstaðir, one of the three parts of the Reykjavik Art Museum, where the painter Jóhannes S. Kjarval occupies a wing.

Jóhannes Kjarval

Kjarval (1885-1972) occupies a particular place in Icelanders' hearts. In his lifetime he was considered the nation's greatest artist, while he was also an unorthodox character and a wit whose *bons mots* are still remembered today. Once in Paris with some friends, he bet with them that all café waiters in the French capital were called Oli (pronounced Oley), before calling to a *garçon*, "un café, au lait!" The waiter understood at once.

Kjarval (his real name was Jóhannes Sveinsson) was born in a farm in the south of the country in 1885 but at the age of five was adopted by a relative who took him to live in Reykjavik, where he took his first drawing lessons. After secondary school he found work as a fisherman for several years before travelling abroad in 1911, to London first and then to Copenhagen where, like many Icelandic artists, he married a Danish woman, whom he later divorced in 1922. He then made various other journeys outside Iceland, notably to Paris. It was not long before he gained recognition. His greatest works were studies of nature painted at Þingvellir and at the Snæfellsnes peninsula.

In the last years of his life Kjarval was respected, admired and famous. The authorities wished to reward him for his artistic contribution and built a villa for him at the seaside, but they had misjudged the artist who refused the gift. Kjarval died in 1972 in Reykjavik.

While his inter-war contemporaries were concerned with social issues in paintings of work in the fields or of seafarers, Kjarval concentrated on nature. If his precursors had revealed the grandiose nature of the country's landscape, he tried to evoke its intimacy. His attention was drawn to the details of the natural world—lava, rocks, lichens—which he rendered in colours that transformed the subjects. Kjarval was the first painter to focus on Iceland's geological complexity, on its lava rocks in particular, which had hitherto been ignored, and his prolific mix of realism and surrealism, which underwent several changes of style, is a permanent source of pleasure. According to the Reykjavik Art Museum:

> Before his death in 1972 the painter Jóhannes Kjarval donated a large collection of his work to the city of Reykjavik. This collection consisted largely of sketches, drawings as well as paintings and several personal belongings of the artist. This donation was the main motivation for the making of Kjarvalstaðir which was inaugurated in 1973. From the beginning the intention was to devote one exhibition hall to the work of Kjarval. Throughout the years the Kjarval collection has grown considerably by acquisitions and by generous gifts by individuals. It now consists of 3348 works, 3189 drawings and 159 paintings.

The recently deceased writer Thor Vilhjalmsson provided this portrait of Kjarval:

> Kjarval was a complete artist, a genius. He ploughed his furrow, made up for the time lost over the centuries, avenged all the generations to whom art and painting was forbidden and did the work of ten men. He taught Icelanders to see what was around them, the ubiquitous drama of their country. He originated the close-up, opening eyes to what is large, harsh and impressive. He made his contemporaries look afresh at this country full of contrasts, which has made us familiar with its excesses, its violence, its gentleness. Kjarval was amazingly productive during his long life. We do not know the precise extent of his work as it is scattered throughout the country. Treasures are to be found in the modest farms where he left them, with poor folk who had warmly welcomed this exceptional

man. With Munch he is a figurehead of Scandinavian art. He would sleep when he was tired, eat when he was hungry, and could not bear the emptiness of routine. Big and strong, every inch an actor, he was master of repartee and often hid his extreme sensitivity behind behaviour that would disconcert his interlocutors if they refused to play along with his sense of imaginative fantasy.

Art by the Sea

For a small city Reykjavik has no shortage of museums and galleries, and several of these are situated close to the sea, the source of so much artistic inspiration. Hafnarhús (Harbour House), a former warehouse situated on the waterfront, is the part of the Reykjavik Art Museum dedicated to contemporary art, and every year an exhibition is organized around an aspect of the work of the postmodern Icelandic Pop Art master Erró whose work is also on permanent display. The Reykjavik Museum of Photography in a next-door building presents both historical and contemporary images of the capital and the country and emphasizes the importance of photography in Icelandic popular culture.

From here it is a short walk to Harpa, the concert hall and conference centre essentially used for music but whose structure is itself a work of art. In winter and summer alike the great modernist building is filled with shifting patterns of light, largely due to the irregular and coloured glass panels designed by the Icelandic-Danish artist Olafur Eliasson.

The Sculpture & Shore Walk takes the visitor past a collection of outdoor sculptures in a parkland setting that culminates in the impressive *Sólfarið* (Sun Voyager), Jón Gunnar Árnason's (1931-89) stainless steel tribute to a mythic longboat facing west and symbolizing a journey into the unknown. Those interested in avant-garde art may want to cross the road to visit Nýló (the Living Art Museum) on Skúlagata, a centre for contemporary visual arts. Continuing along the shoreline, however, leads to the Sigurjón Ólafsson Museum, an institution celebrating the work of the Icelandic sculptor where modernist pieces are exhibited both inside and outside. A few hundred metres away the Ásmundur Sveinsson Sculpture Museum, the third part of the Reykjavik Art Museum, houses the works of Ásmundur Sveinsson (1893-1982), a pioneer sculptor who was inspired by the sagas and Nordic mythology before turning to abstraction.

The Phallus Museum

By no means abstract and crudely figurative, the exhibits at the Icelandic Phallological Museum on Laugavegur attract curious visitors, but those expecting erotic stimulation will be disappointed as the male organs preserved in formaldehyde or dried tend to have the opposite effect. All the mammals to be found in Iceland or in its waters are represented, and there is even one human penis donated by an eccentric libertine who left it to the museum in the hope that his girlfriends would come and pay posthumous homage.

The whale penises are likely to create an inferiority complex among even the best-endowed but the most interesting exhibits are those of creatures whose genitals are entirely retractable like an airplane's wheels—no doubt a defence mechanism against the cold and a way of increasing aerodynamic efficiency. Also of note are those mammals provided by nature with a bone in the middle of their penis, evidence that all animals are not equal.

Theatre

For many years Lutheran Protestantism and theatre were more or less incompatible, and theatrical performances in Iceland were rare. If in other parts of Scandinavia foreign troupes put on plays in French, German or Italian, there was little scope for such activities in Reykjavik. Matthías Jochumsson (1835-1920), the author of the national anthem, is the only playwright of the nineteenth century whose works are still performed today. Jóhann Sigurjónsson (1880-1919) was the greatest dramatist at the beginning of the following century, and his romantic dramas, inspired by Icelandic history, still move local audiences. His best known works are *Galdra Loftur* and *Fjalla Eyvindur*, the former based on a popular tale set in the eighteenth century in which Loftur, whose fiancée Steinunn is pregnant, falls in love with the Devil's daughter and eventually gives himself up to the Devil and dies. *Fjalla Eyvindur*, also a historical piece, tells of the lives of outlaws living in the remote mountains. Reykjavik finally experienced a minor theatrical boom in the 1890s with the construction of theatre building at the Iðnó (Craftsmen's House), built by Tjörnin in 1896-97 and then the founding of the Reykjavik Theatre Company in 1897, performing in Iðnó.

Two dramatists have dominated Reykjavik's theatre scene over the last forty years and both reflect how society has evolved in that time. In the 1970s and 1980s the prolific Kjartan Ragnarsson (b.1945) wrote comedies and dramas that appealed to Icelandic audiences' historical self-conception as a naive, carefree, hard-drinking but ultimately united people. During the same period Birgir Sigurðsson (b.1937) was producing plays that were darker but which also mirrored aspects of national history. Since the 1990s, however, Icelandic society has become more critical, more complex and distanced from the sense of togetherness that followed independence. The unifying and unconsciously patriotic perspective of the preceding generation can appear outdated.

Ólafur Haukur Símonarson (b.1947) has been a major figure in the last two decades with dramas that are pessimistic and sometimes cynical in which typically a family tyrant is finally called to account by his oppressed wife or by his rebellious children. The defeat of the ageing patriarch can be read as a parable of the "old" Iceland, which has kept its culture intact but must give way to modernity. Símonarson's *Hafið* (the Sea) was a big success in Iceland's theatre and was subsequently made into a film by Balthasar Kormákur (b.1966).

Traditionally Icelandic fiction has been adapted into drama, and Laxness' novels have often received this treatment. But if this still occurs, there are now a greater number of original plays, with dark dramas especially popular. The well-known formula often involves a small, remote fishing village and sometimes plays on the taboo theme of incest and abuse. Hidden family secrets, the tedium of life far from the capital, the lure of emigration, the temptations of modern consumerism, nostalgia for lost childhood and the frustrations of a wasted life: these are the main themes. In a less sombre vein, authors such as Bragi Ólafsson (b.1962) and Ragnar Bragason (b.1971) have produced work, both in theatre and cinema, in the form of subtle comedy that verges on the absurd.

Icelanders go to the theatre a great deal, a fact long explained by the relative absence of an Icelandic cinema industry. Films in general are shown in English and all films are subtitled except those for children which are dubbed. Yet even though in recent years a significant number of films have been made in Icelandic, people continue to flock to the theatre, mostly to the National Theatre of Iceland and the modern City Theatre in Reykjavik but also to other independent venues in the capital or to amateur performances in the countryside.

Icelandic Cinema

Cinema in Iceland is a recent phenomenon and is generously subsidized by a tax on cinema tickets. The relative fall in production costs has resulted in a greater number of feature films and now the appearance of an Icelandic film is no longer a special event, and revenues for individual productions have even fallen as cinemagoers have a wider choice of films. Feature films had already been made in Iceland, but the first entirely Icelandic production was the 1977 *Morðsaga* (*Story of a Crime*), the one and only work of director Reynir Oddsson. The film has not stood the test of time and, like many Icelandic dramas, deals with the issue of incest.

A new generation of directors, trained abroad, were meanwhile waiting their turn. Aged around twenty in 1968 and from different backgrounds, they were so few in number that at the beginning they formed something of a closed circle that shared out, often due to political connections, the subsidies available for local productions. The directors' situation was relatively enviable; even if producing a film can be an uphill struggle, as the Nordic countries financed several productions as did the European Union with its Eurimages programme. And above all Icelanders went to see Icelandic films, which is no longer the case today, as family outings, men in suit and tie with grandparents and children. It was almost a sense of duty that drove audiences to see the latest film, as well as the shock of hearing Icelandic and not English spoken in a cinema and seeing familiar landscapes in new and exciting ways. Yet Icelandic cinema was both too rich and too poor: too rich because it quickly exhausted promising talent by allowing directors to make their next film too quickly; too poor to allow big and ambitious productions.

The first feature length films drew audiences of between 50,000 and 100,000, and there were between two and four each year. Between 2000 and 2010, however, when many more films were released, the total audience for all films each year was less than 100,000. Great book buyers, theatre and music lovers, Icelanders are not cinema enthusiasts, and success must be sought overseas.

European assistance, however, had unintended consequences. Co-production criteria meant that foreign actors had to be employed and there was a time when every screen couple had one actor from the co-producing nation—a phenomenon known as the "European pudding". Meanwhile, if public aid to the Icelandic cinema industry is justified by the international publicity it brings, sceptics ask what sort of image of Iceland is transmitted internationally and whether this is more often than not a stereotype. Most Icelandic films that have enjoyed success at film festivals certainly fit a certain format: the action takes place in the countryside and not Reykjavik, nature plays a big part, and the characters suffer from varying degrees of boredom. Such is the cliché—Iceland is a spectacular place where people must be spectacularly bored, especially in winter. Most Icelandic films duly follow this formula, even the best of them, *Noi Albinoi*, which won many awards. Here the film takes place in a village in the western fjords where a strange boy, excluded from school, grows up on the margins of the community between an eccentric grandmother and an alcoholic father until an avalanche dramatically changes life in the village. This poetic film, both tender and cruel, was the first by the director Dagur Kári.

Friðrik Þór Friðriksson, Ágúst Guðmundsson, Hilmar Oddsson and Þorsteinn Jónsson have all made interesting films. Those set in Viking times were a speciality in the 1980s, and producers from the land of the sagas could arguably express the violence of the Vikings better than their Scandinavian colleagues, but the genre was soon exhausted.

Not only the actors but also the very action of films could be largely determined by potential foreign markets. Björn Norðfjörð analyzed this issue in an article on Icelandic cinema published in a book *The Cinema of Small Nations*. Looking at the career of Balthasar Kormákur from *101 Reykjavik* onwards, he observes:

> The narrative of Hallgrímur Helgason's novel, on which the film is based, has been systematically altered in order to accommodate a foreign audience. Most importantly, the nationality of Lola was changed from Icelandic to Spanish. As a result, extensive portions of the film are in English, and the character becomes a stand-in for foreign audience members as Lola is guided around Reykjavik and introduced to local customs . . . In adapting the play *The Sea* (*Hafið*) by Ólafur Haukur Símonarson in 2002, Balthasar Kormákur again reverted to his narrative strategy when he changed the Icelandic character Lóa to the French character of Françoise (Hélène de Fougerolles) who is introduced to local specificities in English. His third feature, *A Little Trip to Heaven*, was an Icelandic film in an industrial sense only, for while it was shot in Iceland it was a noir-ish thriller set in the American Midwest, starring Forest Whitaker and Julia Styles.

The author adds that the director's next film, *The Jar City*, adapted from a novel by Arnaldur Indriðason and thus much more "Icelandic", was one of the country's biggest box office successes—perhaps because it was "marketed as a Hollywood blockbuster".

A Selection of Films

Icelandic films can be found on DVD. We shall avoid those already mentioned and suggest several films classified by genre.

Nature:

The Beast (1986)

Helgi, a young man who dreams of becoming an author, returns with his girlfriend to his childhood home, planning to shoot one last reindeer. It was here that his mother ran off with a German scientist. Director: Hilmar Oddsson.

Children of Nature (1991)
An old man who lives by himself decides to give up farming and move to the city. He meets an old flame in an old people's home and they flee together in search of adventure. Director: Friðrik Þór Friðriksson

Village life:
Nói Albínói (2003)
See above. Director: Dagur Kári

Vikings:
When the Raven Flies (1984)
A new concept of the Viking features the revenge of "Gestur", an Irishman who as a child witnessed the murder of his parents by two Norwegian Vikings. Director: Hrafn Gunnlaugsson

Outlaw, the Saga of Gísli (1981)
Vésteinn, Gísli Súrsson's sworn brother, is murdered. Gísli believes the murderer is Þorgrímur, married to Þórdís, Gísli's sister. Nobody understands the story, including Icelandic pupils who must learn this medieval saga in elementary school. Director: Ágúst Guðmundsson

Thriller:
Deep Winter (1985)
At last a film which takes place during the winter night. A young widow who has been living abroad comes to stay with her in-laws on an isolated farm. She is threatened by unknown persons or forces. Director: Þráinn Bertelsson

Politics:
Ingaló (1992)
The only Icelandic political fiction film, featuring eighteen-year-old Ingaló, who lives with her parents and her younger brother. Studies the condition of people working on a fishing boat and in a fish freezing plant. Director: Ásdís Thoroddsen

Ge9n (2011)
A documentary about the nine people prosecuted for "attacking" Parliament on 8 December 2008 and a radical critique of Icelandic society. Director: Haukur Már Helgason

Musical:

On Top (1982)

Two rock groups, one male, the other female, decide to make a combined effort to be famous by doing a show together. The *Los Angeles Times* reportedly thought: "*On Top* features a bunch of Icelandic fruitcakes wearing strange clothes." Director: Ágúst Gudmundsson

Icelandic Humour:

The Icelandic Dream (2000), *A Man like Me* (2002), *Eleven Men Out* (2005)

Of part Northern Irish parentage, director Robert Ingi Douglas has successfully explored Icelandic humour through themes dealing with racism and homophobia—though they may not always be intelligible to foreigners.

A Children's Film:

Sky Palace (1994)

Emil, an eight-year-old boy, wants to buy a puppy. He works hard to earn the money, but his father rejects the idea. He decides to leave home. Director: Þorsteinn Jónsson

Singing in the Snow

Icelanders like to sing, perhaps as a way of expressing feelings and emotions that they otherwise repress in their horror of *væmið* or anything sentimental. Much has been written about the Americanization of Iceland, about its acceptance of American culture, especially in its televised forms, but the Icelandic mindset is in fact the polar opposite of the American equivalent when it comes to its dislike for sentimentality—except in songs. Most music nowadays is confined almost exclusively to the tastes of younger generations, but the build-up to the annual Eurovision Song Contest offers the opportunity to revisit a sort of music that might have been written in the 1960s. The competition is watched by (almost) everybody and the streets of Reykjavik are empty on that evening as excited families stuff themselves with junk food in front of their televisions as Iceland invariably finishes sixteenth (it once came second). The tune is generally high-tempo, and as people only have to hear it a few times for it to stick in their heads they find it better and better with each playing and so are amazed that a tuneless song (those they're hearing for the first time) could win. The evening always develops in the same way, as families complain when Scandinavian countries fail to vote maximum points to Iceland while cursing the small Balkan nations who always vote for each other without the slightest moral scruple. Intellectuals from bigger countries find it odd that anyone could get so excited about such a mediocre and futile exercise but from Iceland's point of view there is nothing surprising about the controversies, especially as most people only pretend to be outraged and irony is often at play. Icelandic intellectuals describe themselves as "Eurovision addicts" but only out of bad taste or inverted snobbery. In short, everyone enjoys the Eurovision Song Contest and it is not often that Iceland can compete on equal footing in an international competition.

Choirs are ubiquitous in Iceland, and their popularity is probably due to the fact that they offer people a chance to be together, to wear the same clothes (which never otherwise happens even at school or in the army) and to share the same sense of purity. A Reykjavik inhabitant can choose between a parish choir, a university choir, a choir of people originating from a particular fjord or a male or female choir. Young children have their own choirs as do those at secondary school. These choirs travel widely, sing in churches, are much photographed and have these photos published in newspapers at home. Normally Icelanders are very reserved, keen to give the best impression of themselves and fearful of being *til skammar*, in other words bringing shame on themselves and indirectly on all Icelanders. An Icelander travelling abroad is generally self-conscious, discreet and careful to visit the hairdresser before catching the plane. But with the other members of a choir, singing in public, he or she may lose this self-consciousness and may be more at ease than people from other extrovert societies who might be embarrassed at performing to strangers.

Icelanders also like to sing when drinking, or perhaps more accurately after drinking. All those invited to a party receive a songbook, which nearly always contains the same songs. Here again singing is a way of feeling togetherness, not in a spirit of purity but rather more in the complicity of ribald rhymes and double entendres.

Sprengisandur
Ride on, ride on, race across the black sand
Back with Arnarfell the sun is going down
Evil spirits are sporting in the dark land
Shadows falling on the glacier's crown
Lord, pray lead my horse by your will
For long is the stretch I must travel still.

Every day, just before the 12.20 p.m. news on public radio, listeners are treated to a version of an Icelandic song. The country probably holds the world record for the number of students of opera singing, the boldest trying their luck abroad and some such as Kristján Jóhannsson and Kristinn Sigmundsson making successful careers.

Love
The sun burns the night
Night extinguish day
You are my solace before
And after the sun is away

You delight me before,
And after day starts to rise
Cooling summer's fire
And sun-thaw on winter ice.

Love, if the lyrics of this song are to be believed, could be a major factor in global warming.

Björk Guðmundsdóttir and Icelandic Pop

Pop culture in Iceland is very rich, even with regional variations—which is almost incredible for a country of 320,000 people. Singers from Akureyri in the north were famed for *stuðlög*, tunes both moving and rhythmic, while pop singers from Keflavik who had listened a good deal to the American base's radio station were masters of adapting English and American classics (Gunnar Þórðarson et Rúnar Júlíusson). Political music or avant-garde experimentation was generally to be found in the capital.

Björk Guðmundsdóttir, or just Björk, is without any doubt Iceland's best-known musical export. Born in Reykjavik, she made her first recording at the age of twelve and at sixteen she was singing in bands that came out of Reykjavik's Hamrahlíð college, the post-punk Sugarcubes being the best-known. She then had a solo career starting with the album *Debut* (1993), which was to go platinum in the United States. Her distinctive appearance and behaviour—an elfish face with traces of Inuit combined with disconcerting outbursts and a taste for controversy—fuelled her popularity abroad but perhaps less so in Iceland. Indeed, Icelanders have a complex relationship with Björk, admiring her considerable talent and her international success. But the local girl has perhaps succeeded too much for some, and whereas she once sang at places where people could enter for the price of a drink she now appears at the Harpur concert hall at €75 per ticket. And there is another issue: like Céline Dion from French-speaking Quebec, Björk now sings in English, only occasionally lives in Iceland and is seen as having moved away from her fellow Icelanders. The record she brought out at the end of 2011, *Biophilia*, came only eighth among Iceland's bestsellers, behind much less promoted artists.

Björk has espoused radical politics over the years and has been particularly active in supporting environmental protest, notably the campaign against the Kárahnjúkavirkjun hydro-electric dam in the east of the country. She was also briefly a major attraction at the Cannes Film Festival in 2000 when she starred in Lars von Trier's *Dancer in the Dark*, a film about a Czech immigrant's struggle with poverty and disease in the United States. No longer the unpredictable adolescent of Reykjavik, she remains an inimitable artist and one who has willingly played a major role in promoting Icelandic music in the wider world. Fascinated by her, music lovers have wanted to know more about the country's music and culture, and without her groups such as Múm, GusGus or Sigur Rós, whatever their qualities, would not have had the success they have enjoyed overseas.

Bands are formed, break up and re-form in different guises, and any visitor to Reykjavik will have no trouble hearing live local music. The choice is widest during the autumn Iceland Airwaves festival, held every October and dubbed "the hippest long weekend on the annual music-festival calendar" by *Rolling Stone* magazine. Buying a bracelet, in theory allows festival-goers entrance into any performance, even if the queues are sometimes long and some events are deemed to be sold out. Beyond the festival, however, travellers need only go to a city-centre bar advertising live music to immerse themselves in the country's musical culture. Icelanders are generally late to bed or rather early to bed as sleepless nights hold no fear for them, so whatever time you arrive for the show it is almost certain to be too early.

1 Reykjavik, Iceland's biggest forest (courtesy Visit Reykjavik)

2 Brightly painted houses in winter (Bjørn Giesenbauer/Wikimedia Commons)

3 Ingólfur Arnarson founds Reykjavik by Johan Peter Raadsig (1806-1882) (Haukur Þorgeirsson/Wikimedia Commons)

4 Iceland in Olaus Magnus' Map of Scandinavia 1539 (James Ford Bell Library, University of Minnesota)

5 Icelandic turf house with drying fish, 1835, by Joseph-Paul Gaimard

6 Reykjavik, 1862, by Bayard Taylor (Library of Congress)

7 Reykjavik's prison on Skólavörðurstígur, the first stone building (Guðmundur D. Haraldsson/ Wikimedia Commons)

8 Art Nouveau Höfði, scene of the 1986 Reagan-Gorbachev summit (courtesy Visit Reykjavik)

9 Corrugated iron cladding, Hverfisgata (Christian Bickel/Wikimedia Commons)

10 The *Althing* or parliament (JøMa/Wikimedia Commons)

11 The Landakotskirkja or Catholic cathedral (Christian Bickel/Wikimedia Commons)

12 The Hallgrímskirkja at night (courtesy Visit Reykjavik)

13 The Lutheren Fríkirkjan, dating from 1903 (McKay Savage/Wikimedia Commons)

14 The Harpa concert hall at sunset (Mherronnyc/Wikimedia Commons)

15 Winter view from Perlan (courtesy Visit Reykjavik)

16 Perlan in summer (courtesy Visit Reykjavik)

17 US troops in Iceland, 1943 (army.mil/Wikimedia Commons)

18 Then . . . Keflavik airport in the 1970s (Christian Bickel/Wikimedia Commons)

19 And now . . . the contemporary airport (Eirikur Magnusson/ Wikimedia Commons)

21 Portrait of Halldór Kiljan Laxness, Nobel laureate, by Einar Hákonarson (Wikimedia Commons)

20 Egill, Icelandic hero par excellence (Wikimedia Commons)

22 Hallgrimur Helgason (Forlagið, Reykjavik)

23 Prose edition of Snorri Sturluson's *Prose Edda* (1666)

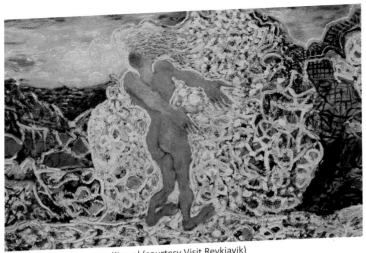

24 Painting by Jóhannes Kjarval (courtesy Visit Reykjavik)

25 Ásmundur Sveinsson Sculpture Museum (TommyBee)

26 *Sólfarið* by Jón Gunnar Árnason (Linda Hilberdink Photography/Shutterstock)

9

27 New Year's fireworks (courtesy Visit Reykjavik)

28 Traditional Icelandic food, including sheep's head (The blanz/ Wikimedia Commons)

29 Icelandic horse Dagur Brynjólfsson/Wikimedia Commons

30 The old Icelandic economy: stockfish (Gunnar Hafdal/ Wikimedia Commons)

31 A remote farming community, north-west Iceland (Thorsteinn Asgeirsson/ Shutterstock)

32 Fishing trawler at harbour, Reykjavik (Vadim Petrakov/Shutterstock)

33 The new Icelandic economy: Landsbankinn headquarters (Christian Bickel/Wikimedia Commons)

34 The ill-fated Icesave advertises in London (Shiny Things/Wikimedia Commons)

35 Icelanders take to the streets of Reykjavik to protest against post-crash austerity, November 2008 (OddurBen/Wikimedia Commons)

36 Icelandic Manhattan?: The financial district of Saebraut (Christian Bickel/Wikimedia Commons)

37 The lighthouse, Seltjarnarnes (Juan Ramon Rodriguez Sosa/Wikimedia Commons)

38 Bessastaðir, the president's residence (Guðlaug Helga Konráðsdótir/Wikimedia Commons)

39 Imagine Peace, memorial to John Lennon (courtesy Visit Reykjavik)

13

40 Eyjafjallajökull erupts, April 2010 (David Karnå/Wikimedia Commons)

41 Esja, the volcanic mountain range, seen from Reykjavik (Christian Bickel/Wikimedia Commons)

42 A meadow of lupins (JuTa/Wikimedia Commons)

43 The Northern Lights (courtesy Visit Reykjavik)

44 The Blue Lagoon (Bloody-libu/Wikimedia Commons)

45 Nesjavellir geothermal plant (Gretar Ívarsson/Wikimedia Commons)

46 Gullfoss Waterfall (Hansueli Krapf/Wikimedia Commons)

47 Þingvellir National Park (Ivan Sabljak/Wikimedia Commons)

48 Strokkur (The Churn) (Chris 73/Wikimedia Commons)

7 | Leisure and Pleasure
Popular Culture and Pastimes

Icelanders have only recently had time to take time off. For many years they did more work than anyone else in Europe: 51 hours a week on average for men and 45 hours for women. Now, of course, the economic crisis has changed everything and overtime is no longer the rule but the exception. And yet certain types of behaviour persist, leading some to wonder how a people who worked so much could be so creative and, at the same time, how they manage not to look more tired than they do. Icelanders were even for a long time world leaders in male longevity and second in female, but life expectancy has stalled for some time now at the same time as the working week has shortened—which seems to defy a process of cause and effect. It seems, however, that the explanation lies in the fact that the country has never known war and that Icelandic women, liberated earlier than their Latin sisters, began to smoke heavily in the 1940s with the arrival of British troops. If the exceptional longevity of people in southern Europe can be explained by a spectacular reduction in alcoholism, the same can also apply to Icelanders, already among the lightest drinkers in Europe even if some do their best to give the opposite impression.

Icelanders have a relationship with time that allows them to rest and recuperate: it is not uncommon to sleep until midday and later on Saturday and Sunday. They have inherited a flexible notion of time and work, an ability to be on call, to work when work is needed. In the fishing industry, for instance, work has to be done when fish are in the nets, while in the fish processing plants it was unthinkable to turn down overtime when a trawler might appear with a hundred tons on board and every day counted as fish very quickly loses its value. The situation is different now as lorries refrigerate the fish between trawler and factory or it is frozen on board, and it is now mostly foreign nationals who work in the processing

Football on frozen Tjörnin (courtesy Visit Reykjavik)

plants. But despite all such changes, Icelanders have kept a fluid, malleable concept of time. When they are having fun, a late or even sleepless night is not a problem, and it is quite common after a party with friends to go into town until five or six in the morning and then to have another party elsewhere. Icelanders who dream of the great cities that "never sleep" often return home disappointed, remarking with amazement that "everything closes at midnight". The rhythm of the seasons also calls for a flexible attitude towards time, as a year is not a succession of days and nights but of vastly different periods, as in summer when it is permanently daytime and winter when it is almost always night. Why go to bed early during June when the sun is already rising at the moment other people in Europe are safely asleep? Yet Icelanders' capacity for recuperation does not alone explain the apparent absence of tiredness—lack of pollution is a factor as is the fact that almost nobody travels long distances or commutes by public transport.

Icelandic children enjoy long school holidays, secondary school students having no school between mid-May and mid-August with ten days holiday at Christmas and Easter. Bank holidays, however, are relatively rare and are generally religious in nature such as Ascension Day and Whitsun. The national holiday (Independence, 17 June) and the August bank holiday fall within the school holidays. Iceland was for a long time a rural economy, where parents needed children's help in farm work or in the fish factories. Until the end of last century all newspapers were delivered into letter boxes by children, while in the villages children spent the summer playing together close to the fish factory until a bell alerted them that there was work to do such as preparing langoustines. On Friday afternoons their mothers would go to collect the envelope containing the children's pay. This happened not in the nineteenth century but in 1987, in the village of Djúpivogur in the eastern fjords. European Union employment directives signed by Iceland finally put an end to child labour.

City dwellers were also traditionally sent in the summer to the countryside in order to help with farm work in return for which farmers would offer board and lodging and a little pocket money. Sending a child to the country was widely considered a form of civic education and the financial aspect was secondary, with many children returning each year to the same farmers who became a second family. Yet such has been the decline in the number of Iceland's farms (there are about 2,000 left) that sending children from Reykjavik to the country has become almost impossible, especially as manual agricultural labour is no longer valued with the advent of mechanization. Yet young people continue to work in the summer or in the evenings or at weekends, and not working is very much the exception to the rule. For those with no contacts who have failed to find a job, the city authorities guarantee two or three weeks' paid work in community schemes such as park and garden maintenance.

Sport

Sport is a way for small nations to compete with bigger ones and every team has a chance, even if sporting contests are rarely a lottery and the best usually win. As there are so few Icelanders their

119

prospects of winning anything are mathematically remote—with the notable exception of handball, a sport that arouses the country's patriotic fervour. The world and European championships and the Olympic Games are key moments in Iceland's sporting life as it is then that the country is a true competitor in the field of handball. Preparations are made months in advance as the population is invited to contribute towards the travelling expenses of the national team, which has its own anthem. When the Icelandic team came second in the 2008 Olympic Games to the French their returning plane swooped low over the capital, they were greeted by the president of the republic and processed into the centre of Reykjavik surrounded by jubilant, flag-waving crowds, leaving commentators wondering what would have happened if they had won.

Handball's success in Iceland is perhaps unsurprising as it is a popular sport in Germany and Scandinavia, where small towns that cannot support a major football club take pride in their local team. As an indoor sport it can be played all year round whatever the weather and as a game of intense physical contact it seems to appeal to the Icelandic temperament. More significantly, it offers the best players the chance to pursue a professional career in Scandinavia or Germany (in 2012 nine out of the sixteen-man national squad were employed in Germany, and three in Denmark). Without being truly professionals, players who remain in Iceland are largely supported by the national organization. Other popular indoor sports are badminton and basketball, while *glíma*, Icelandic wrestling, has no more than 350 contestants in the country.

One outdoor sport, however, has grown in popularity over the last few years: golf. Every village in Iceland has its own golf course, even if rudimentary, and the capital boasts several including Reykjavik Golf Club, which was founded in the 1930s. In Iceland the sport is not a sign of social distinction or a source of snobbery and all sorts of people play, but particularly the retired. Golf's democratic credentials are probably due to the fact that most courses are under-subscribed and are relatively cheap to use. Because of its seasonal nature (golf can be played at night in summer but hardly at all in winter) charter flights to warmer golf courses in Spain or Tunisia are usually fully booked.

The sport of choice, however, is—as anywhere else—football, and no Sunday worthy of its name passes without English football games broadcast on national television. Icelanders bet on Premier League games, generally support a particular team and go to London to watch Chelsea or Arsenal while their wives go shopping in Oxford Street. As for the Icelandic national team, it has trouble rising above 100th place in the FIFA world rankings and almost always loses, only finding satisfaction with even smaller nations like the Faroe Islands, San Marino or Liechtenstein. Understandably, Icelanders have developed a true culture of failure as the history of matches with almost any country is invariably a list of humiliating defeats. The national team always announces imperturbably that it is playing to win, and supporters hope that unusually cold and foul weather will demoralize the opposition—before the inevitable defeat. Yet defeat in Iceland leaves no scars, as it has been so much anticipated, pre-digested, that it creates no bitterness in discussions the next day at work.

Icelandic players, many of whom are professionals in Norway, Denmark and Sweden as well as Britain, can command high transfer fees and their exploits are closely followed in the national press. But these same players, when called upon to inspire and lead the national team, never perform miracles. Disappointed perhaps by the repeated shortcomings of their players, growing numbers of Icelanders have resorted in recent years to women's football as in the United States. Statistics show that two-thirds of registered players nationally are men and one third women.

The West Ham Adventure

Icelanders have always dreamed of owning an English football club. A consortium of rich trawler owners from the Westmann Islands bought Stoke City FC in the 1990s and briefly appointed an Icelandic manager but the club stagnated and soon became a financial liability, with the Icelandic investors relieved to part company with the club. The Icelandic billionaire tycoon Björgólfur

Guðmundsson, who controlled Iceland's main bank Landsbanki, was not deterred by this example and was even more ambitious. According to Jón F. Thoroddsen's *On Thin Ice*:

Guðmundsson achieved some notoriety in the UK when he bought the London football team West Ham United in November 2006 for 108 million pounds. Guðmundsson, a long-time football enthusiast, owned a 95 percent share and his partner Eggert Magnússon, a biscuit factory owner and former president of the Football Association of Iceland, owned a 5 percent share and became Chairman of the club.

Their goal was to make West Ham one of England's best teams in just a few years and to make it to the Champions League. West Ham was in danger of relegation when the Icelanders bought the team, in addition to having contractual difficulties with Media Sports Investments, the company holding the rights to star players Carlos Tevez and Javier Mascherano. The Icelandic owners got off to a good start: West Ham miraculously escaped relegation and won an away game against Manchester United in the final game of the season.

When it was clear that West Ham would remain in the Premier League, the Icelandic owners began hunting for new players to strengthen the squad. Freddie Ljungberg was brought in from Arsenal and became the team's highest paid player. Ljungberg named Magnússon as the main reason for his move, stating that he liked his plan. Defender Lucas Neill also decided to move to West Ham, despite an offer from Liverpool FC, explaining that he and the Icelanders thought along similar lines. The fact that West Ham offered him twice as much money as Liverpool might have had something to do with his decision. Other players bought by the Icelanders included Scott Parker, Craig Bellamy and Matthew Upson.

The Icelanders weren't just passionate football fans. They also had ambitious ideas on how to profit from ownership of the team, and proposed to tear down Upton Park, West Ham's home ground, in order to use the valuable land to build expansive real estate there. West Ham's home games were to be played at the London Olympic Stadium, under construction for the 2012 games. These plans were dropped after meetings with London Mayor Boris Johnson proved unsuccessful.

On 13 December 2007, Eggert Magnússon sold his shares to Guðmundsson, who then took over as a Chairman. In an interview with *The Guardian*, published that same day, he was as ambitious as ever:

Guðmundsson now wants to push ahead with a move to a new £250m, 60,000-seater stadium—a site has been identified at an old Parcelforce depot next to West Ham tube station. "We are seeking to build some truly solid foundations for the future ambitions of West Ham United FC," he said. "This is a great football club with tremendous heritage and tradition and the most wonderful set of supporters. My job as owner is to help plan for the future and create the right conditions off the field to help Alan Curbishley and the playing squad deliver success on the field."

This, like so many plans of the Icelandic bankers, was not to be. In June 2009, CB Holding owned by the resolution committee of Staumur-Burðarás Investment Bank, took over West Ham and Björgólfur Guðmundsson disappeared from the world of English football. In January 2010, David Gold and David Sullivan acquired a majority share in the club, and in February 2011, West Ham United was finally selected as the preferred club to move into the Olympic Stadium after the 2012 Games. Despite this morale-boosting news, West Ham still had to face relegation the following May.

Winter Sports and Water

One might expect Icelanders to excel at winter sports and swimming, but this is not the case as the country has a mild Atlantic climate, all major settlements are close to the sea and skiing is hardly practicable, especially close to Reykjavik. When there is snow bad weather and storms very often prevent access to the pistes, and when the weather is fine there is unlikely to be sufficient snow. Even though winters can be harsh, it can be hard to find good skiing around the capital, where lifts are almost at sea level and slopes are far from steep. The situation is different in the north where the inhabitants of

Akureyri, Dalvík or Siglufjörður enjoy skiing throughout the winter. There is an indoor skating rink in Reykjavik, but most amateur skaters prefer Tjörnin, the lake in the town centre, even if each fall of snow means that the surface must be cleared. Snowmobiles are popular but dangerous, while ice hockey also has a following (Iceland was rated 36th in the world in 2011). Perhaps climatic peculiarities are to blame for Icelanders' lack of enthusiasm for winter sports, but there may be a deeper reason: the absence of a culture of cold, which has already been mentioned, and the way in which people prefer to ignore the climate in which they live.

Icelanders, on the other hand, love swimming and swimming pools. Some swim an impressive number of lengths, while others are happy with a sauna or outdoor geothermal hot tubs from which they emerge tired but happy, even in winter, to expose their bodies to the open air. Some regulars meet every day in the same hot tub and discuss current affairs, while sitting in a circle in water of more than 40°C people are inclined to talk to strangers. Bathers take turns to have their backs massaged or move from a hot tub to a cooler one or vice-versa.

Most Icelanders suffer from an excess of socialization. Social circles include: the extended family, most of whom are nearby if one lives in Reykjavik; the old friends from primary and secondary school and university; acquaintances from choir, from the gym, members of a particular club and their wives; work colleagues; and fellow members of the trade union, professional organization or political party. Meeting all these people is inevitable and quite often compulsory, for it is not allowed to miss a birthday, a first communion or a funeral. Not surprisingly, Icelanders yearn for the anonymity and freedom that they discover when travelling abroad. But the public bath also offers a sort of freedom because it is a place of sociability and conviviality, free from the obligations of pre-existing social networks. One leaves one's clothes in the changing rooms without fear that they will be stolen and heads for the shower, naked and in full view of other bathers. A very explicit poster indicates which parts of the body should be carefully washed before entering the water: armpits, feet, but also

124

genitals. On leaving one showers again, this time to remove traces of chlorine, in naturally hot water.

Great fans of swimming pools, Icelanders are nonetheless not great swimming champions, faring badly in Scandinavian and other competitions. This lack of swimming prowess may be due to the temperature of the water; at an average 28°C it is noticeably warmer than elsewhere in Europe and tends to encourage relaxation and wallowing rather than the urge to fight the cold through exertion.

The sea is too cold for swimming and only attracts those interested in extreme sports. But the Reykjavik authorities have come up with an ingenious system at the so-called geothermal beach at Nauthólsvik (accessible by bus), which allows swimmers to get close to the sea. An almost closed bay whose waters flow into the Atlantic has been dredged and deepened, and surplus hot water from the municipal geothermal system is pumped into a small, quite hot pool and also into the bay itself, which is considerably colder. Some of the braver swimmers are thus able to practise a few strokes in the sea without dying of hypothermia. A sand beach has been developed, and Nauthólsvik is popular with families in summer. Since the crisis of 2008, however, it has also been increasingly popular with some who go to swim there in the winter—as if to prove to themselves that self-discipline and meeting a challenge are more important than dreaming of a distant Caribbean beach.

The Icelandic Horse

Unlike golf, horse riding is a sign of social status—but not in the countryside where every farmer has at least a couple of horses. These small animals may look like ponies—and no visitor should refer to them as such—but they are tough and long-lived and have a unique ambling gait known as the *tölt*. In winter the Icelandic horse can be left outside provided he is supplied with hay, where he will bow his head in the storm, point his croup towards the wind and wait for the good weather to return with endless patience. Horses have chestnut, white or grey coats, not very different from the colouring of local sheep. They boast magnificent manes, and their hides make superb bedside rugs.

Reykjavik dwellers with horses often own land on a former farm but in winter they keep their animals in horse boxes near to the city. All this is a costly business, and many farmers who take care of city people's horses have benefitted from a substantial extra income. Horses also enjoy a special status in Icelandic culture, not shared by other animals. Sheep are often criticized for damaging the environment, but nobody would dream of pointing out the harm done by horses whose owners are usually middle-class professionals with impeccable green credentials. This points to a deep and ancient love of horses in Iceland, where breeding, competitions and prizes are all big business. For centuries the horse was the only means of transport on land, but now it represents a leisure activity like golf, less strenuous than walking and inseparable from group sociability. Riders set off together on excursions, enjoy a sing-song in the evening and a drink in convivial society. An activity that can be mixed, it is nevertheless underpinned by an exclusively masculine culture that is not to everybody's taste.

Chess

There are some collective passions that seem to define a people and promise to last forever, and yet they disappear once the conditions that lay at the origins no longer exist. Such is the case with chess in Iceland, a game from the Orient that Icelanders once loved as it suited their temperament perfectly. It is a game, for instance, that can be played for hours on end without speaking—no doubt less attractive to Latin nations—and it can be played with a clear head or in an alcoholic stupor. It is a game where the contestant measures himself directly against his adversary (in Iceland it is a predominantly masculine pastime, and mixed competitions are rare) without a display of muscle power. The game is individual but also collective when a number of chess boards are involved in a competition.

Icelanders developed an international reputation as chess experts from the founding in 1925 of the Icelandic Chess Federation and in 1972 the country was rewarded with hosting the World Chess Championship between Boris Spassky (the "Russian bear") and the tortured American genius Bobby Fischer. With a background of Cold War tension, the 24-game contest was held in the Laugardalshöll arena in Reykjavik and lasted from 11 July to 31 August, at which point Spassky admitted defeat and Fischer ended 24 years of Soviet world domination in the game.

This was the high point of chess in Iceland and interest was so acute that a newspaper in Reykjavik subscribed to an international news agency solely to obtain news of chess matches around the world. The stars of international chess were household names in Iceland, where photographers would expectantly wait at the airport if a competition was to be held on the island. All matches were accompanied by commentary on peak-time radio and television, while chess was an integral part of the school curriculum. The table at which Spassky and Fischer had played was exhibited with reverence for years in the National Museum of Iceland. Iceland's chess masters, treated as civil servants, received professorial salaries.

The two unwitting combatants in the Cold War "Match of the Century" were not what the world had wanted to make of them. Boris Spassky was remarried to a French woman and the hero of the Soviet Union went to live in France. The unpredictable Fischer renounced his Jewish background and converted to a Christian sect, disappeared for years before resurfacing as an advocate of Serbia in the Balkan civil war. In 2005, after a series of controversies in which his anti-Israel and anti-US stance hardened, Iceland's parliament voted for him to be granted Icelandic citizenship after he was threatened with deportation by Japan. He lived a largely reclusive life in Reykjavik until his death in 2008.

Enthusiasm for chess in Iceland was a collateral victim of the collapse of the Soviet Union, as the status of dissident enjoyed by Victor Korschnoi and attributed to Garry Kasparov no longer had any meaning. Nor was Iceland the front line in international chess politics against Soviet might. It hardly mattered any more whether Icelandic masters won or lost, and international competitions, now featuring hungry Russian immigrants, were less lavishly funded. The Icelandic national team decided to shelter under the banner of the national shipping line Eimskip in order to refill its depleted coffers, while in an unwittingly suicidal gesture all the players—except

Hannes Hlífar Stefánsson, who continued to shine as a grand-master—declared their support for the conservative politician and prime minister Davíð Oddsson. From that point onwards, chess in Iceland entered a dramatic decline as people looked elsewhere for idols without such obvious feet of clay.

One such idol, who was also destined to fall, was Jón Páll Sigmarsson, a bodybuilder and strongman who won the World's Strongest Man title four times between 1984 and 1990. He had first won an award in a contest organized by a lorry firm, encouraging a large number of imitators who competed in various contests with titles such as Iceland's Strongest Viking. There was initially little open discussion of steroid abuse, and the devastating effect of performance enhancing drugs was not yet understood. The blond giant Jón Páll, a true Nordic icon, was a nightclub bouncer by night and trained in a gym named Jakaból (giants' nest) during the day. Pushed by the urge to win but also by the expectations of his admirers, he resorted to steroids to build his spectacular physique. After a decade of success he died suddenly in his Reykjavik gym in January 1993 of a heart attack at the age of thirty-two. Some claimed that his ruptured aorta was the result of steroid abuse, while others maintained that it was a hereditary health problem. In any case he was finally laid low by the body he had so arduously built, leaving behind a cult of extreme bodybuilding.

Holidays

Getting together in Iceland takes two main forms, one purely social and the other more ritualistic and even mystical. The latter is what happens on the evening of 24 December. The sitting room has been repainted, the apartment cleaned from top to toe, the children are in the Sunday best with polished shoes, everybody has taken a bath—and finally six o'clock arrives. The street outside is deserted, for the time is full of significance: Christmas dinner can begin. Once this annual feast was finished inside half an hour in traditional rural Iceland, but nowadays in Reykjavik it is surrounded by gastronomic pretensions and social niceties. Until recently most Icelanders would only eat pork once a year at Christmas, and cooked in the

Danish fashion with crackling, but now lamb is just as popular, highly smoked (in horse manure for the purists) and accompanied by caramelized potatoes and reconstituted dried peas. Today frozen peas are in daily use but at Christmas the tinned "Ora" brand of peas (sold confusingly as *grænar baunir* of green beans) are a must. If any Icelander is unfortunate enough to have to spend a Christmas abroad, friends or relatives will certainly be willing to save the day by sending a can. Some prefer their meat lightly smoked, which goes under the name of London lamb.

Icelanders tend to disappear until 31 December, stuffing themselves with biscuits baked in December and chocolate and reading the books they have received as gifts. Christmas had already started for the children on 11 December with the appearance of the first of the thirteen Icelandic Father Christmases who live in the mountains with their mother, Grýla, a dreadful ogress, and their father Leppalúði. They come down into town one by one each day up to 24 December and leave in the same order in the days leading to Epiphany on 6 January. Children place a shoe on a window sill each evening and hope to find a treat or a small toy when they wake up, and this goes on for almost a fortnight. Those who have not been good may find a potato instead, so few are inclined to misbehave in the run-up to Christmas. There are variations of the tradition outside Reykjavik; some villages have no fewer than 24 Father Christmases, while one—because of the meanness of its inhabitants, it is said—has only nine.

New Year's Eve is an occasion that all Icelanders love, perhaps because it represents the fusion between wanting to share in a communal moment of celebration and the dream of individual freedom. The evening starts with bonfires, normally situated at the seaside, which provide an ideal opportunity to get rid of anything that will burn. Some people sing, others drink and most do both. After a few minutes the spectators abandon the bonfires to settle in front of the television and watch the satirical review of the year's events. The programme is never really malicious as its producers are careful not to criticize any political party more than its opponents, and as a result the attempt to create satire without hurting anyone's feelings can be slightly distressing. As the credits roll everybody then gets ready for the next stage of the celebration—the fireworks, nowadays a semi-professional, stage-managed event with displays of pyrotechnic precision. What is truly Icelandic about the spectacle is not the fireworks themselves but how individualism and collective behaviour manifest themselves. Everybody does exactly the same thing at the same moment, and yet the whole is made up of a series of individual actions and gestures. Families, all generations together, go into their garden, onto their balcony or onto the open space in front of the church where rapidly, if there is little wind, a thick cloud of smoke conceals both people and fireworks. Before the economic crisis it was accepted behaviour to boast how much the fireworks cost (the profits from which went to voluntary organizations such as search and rescue groups), but now this would be in bad taste. Nevertheless, fireworks in Reykjavik provide a spectacular New Year's Eve show and draw large numbers of tourists each year.

At midnight everyone toasts the New Year, and the night becomes pagan. Children go to bed, parents tidy up and the young go into central Reykjavik to drink, not until dawn—which comes much later at this time of year—but well into the early hours, while late firecrackers explode sporadically (by law the last of these have to be used by 6 January). In years of heavy snowfall the charred remains of fireworks remain buried until April when they are tidied up in the general spring cleaning.

Christmas in Iceland assumes a greater significance than in any country in Northern Europe. Those who are studying abroad always return home for the holiday, even if this is the only time of the year that they can afford to do so. Christmas is also the greatest opportunity to spend money (the crisis notwithstanding) and everything possible is done to help people part with their cash: Christmas bonuses, hire purchase deals and credit—credit card payment demands are specially delayed until the beginning of February for purchases made after 11 December. Yet almost a fifth of all such purchases are made abroad, generally around the end of November, and as with football the preferred country for shopping is Britain.

Þorrablót

Icelanders have a word for winter nights: *skammdegið*. The darkness is at its deepest around the winter solstice on 21 December but the Christmas festivities and their preparation, culminating in light and warmth, help to banish the gloom. It is in January that Icelanders can suffer from depression (perhaps seasonal affective disorder), but also in February and March, when the days have grown longer. The sun only appears over the mountains in February in certain western fjord communities, which gives rise to celebrations. Yet winter darkness is less complete than in the north of Norway and Sweden, with all Icelanders living below the Arctic Circle. Holidays, theatre and concerts allow most to overcome the ambient depression that doctors have studied and which should not in any event be confused with the suicide rate (Iceland came 39th in the 2011 World Health Organization's country ranking). Contrary to received wisdom, suicides occur in spring and not in winter. When everybody is sad, the most depressed, those who are "in the cellar" as the Icelandic idiom has it, feel they are part of the norm. It is when the spring buds reappear, the countryside turns green once more and people begin to feel better again that the truly depressed give up hope.

There is no point in gardening before May. Bulbs imported from Holland insist on flowering at the same time as their counterparts in Amsterdam and are often destroyed by frost, but daffodils (*páskaliljur* or Easter lilies in Icelandic) only flower at the end of May or start of June.

In the struggle against the winter blues a daily dose of cod liver oil is recommended as a tonic, the vitamin D replacing that lost by lack of sunlight. If that does not work, there is always the option of taking part in a *Þorrablót*. Before Christianization the Old Icelandic Calendar defined the period from around 20 January to late February as *Þorri*, and *Þorrablót* was thus a midwinter pagan festival, featuring traditional delicacies conserved in *mysa*, a marinade of fermented sour milk or whey. These treats may include ram's testicles prepared in their own sauce, rotten seals' flippers, whale blubber and sheep's heads complete with eyes that are particularly prized. All these dishes—and more—are served in a form of wooden trough like (it is assumed at least) in Viking times. *Brennivín*, a schnapps flavoured with caraway and popularly known as Black Death, is served ice cold along with dried fish, herrings and for those who are alarmed by such exotic dishes more reassuring items such as smoked salmon (*reyktur lax*) and raw salmon with dill (*graflax*). Very old people rediscover flavours that they had know in their childhood and now only enjoy once a year, while for secret drinkers who do not really like this sort of food the occasion is the pretext for open alcoholic indulgence, and those who only drink once a year are likely to do so at a *Þorrablót*. For younger participants eating this unusual fare is an initiation ceremony, a ritual that allows access into a sense of belonging to the nation. There are some who truly like whale blubber soaked in fermented milk, and then there is the rest of humanity. Even so, these feasts, which seem delightfully ancient, are in fact a relatively recent invention, believed to date back to Icelandic student associations at the end of the nineteenth century and the dawning of a nationalist ideology that romanticized a mythic Viking past. They began to become more widespread when the food that they are meant to celebrate ceased to be part of Icelanders' daily lives.

From Cradle to Grave

Social life is family-based and punctuated by rites of passage: christening, communion, marriage and death. Christening is often surrounded by a certain atmosphere of suspense and Icelandic parents are granted a year in which to decide on the first name of their child, some insisting that it is impossible to select a name before discovering the baby's personality. The name is revealed on the day of the christening itself, chosen from an approved list that was traditionally extremely limited and rigid containing only forenames from the sagas or from the Bible. The forename is then later the base on which the patronym is based, the father's (or mother's) first name in the genitive case and with the suffix *–son* for boys and *–dóttir* for girls. In the past a foreigner who wished to adopt Icelandic nationality had to take a new name and a patronym, but this requirement broke down under the pressure of mixed marriages and European directives but also for another reason. Danish family names had been allowed to co-exist with the patronymic system up to the beginning of the twentieth century. Some of these names originated with real Danish families and others from wealthier, status-seeking Icelandic farmers who had "Danified" the name of the place where they had been born. When under feminist pressure it was conceded that children could take their mother's name, the growth in these family names escalated as they were considered more socially desirable than the overly common patronyms. A man might pass on his family name to his children but if he married a woman with one of these prestigious names they would normally adopt this instead. Those born abroad and the growth of an imported "aristocracy" was beginning to threaten the traditional nomenclature, so it was decided to add another intermediary name, which can be one of these family names or another alluding to the place of birth—but on condition that it be in the dative case. Names then became a sort of linguistic and grammatical obstacle course, with the forename in the nominative, the intermediary eventually in the dative and the patronymic form in the genitive . . .

If communion, religious or secular, is still a highlight in the social ritual, then marriage is less and less so. Funerals, on the other hand, are conducted with the unchanging rhythm of tradition. Deaths are first announced on national radio before the lunchtime and evening news bulletins. Announcements then appear in the newspapers stating the date and place of the funeral service. On the morning of the service the press publishes obituaries or tributes from family, friends or colleagues. The funeral itself, unless the deceased is very old, takes place in a church in the presence of several hundred people and afterwards everybody is invited to a reception in a big hotel. Attending a funeral is nothing short of a right, which no employer would dare to question. And while the occasion is sad for the family of the deceased, it also offers those attending some undeniable pleasures—the chance to socialize and gossip, to stuff themselves with cakes and to get back in advance some of the huge costs of their own funeral.

Social life is also interspersed with annual gatherings and parties (old school friends and work colleagues, club members, those from the same village). An Icelander stays in contact all his or her life with people encountered at different stages, from childhood up to death. The country's entire population is contained within a single telephone directory, and every Icelander contains within his or her head a mental list of about 2,000 names that are refreshed each day by opening the newspaper, listening to the radio or meeting acquaintances at the bakery. This may happen elsewhere in rural communities, but in Iceland and in Reykjavik it happens on a national scale. Those who wish to live without being constantly recognized have to move abroad. And yet at the airport, during those delays that force people together, two Icelanders who have never set eyes on each other will strike up a conversation and by the law of degrees of separation they soon find that they know plenty of people in common.

8

Faith in the City
The Religious Landscape

The Norse Gods

The first Vikings were pagans, sharing the same cosmology as other Scandinavian peoples. They believed in Odin, the ruler of the gods, Tyr, the god of war, Thor, the god of thunder, and Skirnir, the messenger and equivalent of Mercury. They believed that their warriors, courageously killed in combat, would be transported by the Valkyries to Valhalla, "the hall of the slain", the paradise that awaited the brave. The most precious exhibit in the National Museum of Iceland in Reykjavik is a small figure of Thor dating from the Viking era. In the capital streets are named after birds, trees, plants or geographical features that are impossible to translate into English, but the exceptions are those carrying the names of heroes from the sagas and gods of Norse mythology. In an old district in the centre of town are streets in honour of Thor, Tyr and Odin.

Snorri Sturluson (1179-1241), historian, poet and politician, remains the most significant source regarding Norse gods and mythology, and his main work, the *Prose Edda*, deals with issues of language and poetry as well as describing the Norse cosmology. The names of the main Norse gods are more or less familiar, but those of the goddesses are much less so, and their precise characteristics remain obscure.

The most celebrated god was Odin, father of all the gods, called all-father but also Val father (father of the slain) because all those who died in battle were his adopted sons. Thor jealously guarded his hammer Mjölnir, a belt that gave him his strength and his wife Sif, celebrated for her beauty. Baldur, the god of lamentations, the husband of Nanna and the son of Odin and Frigg, was the wisest and purest of all the divinities but also the least able to achieve his goals. Njörd controlled wind, sea and fire, and it was to him that fishermen turned for a successful catch. He had two children, a son

The Hallgrímskirkja (Someone35/Wikimedia Commons)

Freyr and a daughter Freyja, the god of love and fertility. Other important figures were Tyr, god of war, and Loki, a shape shifter and god of trickery.

The names of Norse gods are commonly given to Icelandic children today, although those with negative connotations such as Loki are rarely used. In English, meanwhile, Tuesday is derived from Tyr's day, Wednesday from Odin or Woden's day and Friday from Freyr's day. This does not apply in Icelandic, where Tuesday is simply *þriðjudagur*, the third day, Wednesday *miðvikudagur*, the mid-week day, Friday *föstudagur* or fasting day and Saturday *laugardagur* or washing day.

Snorri Sturluson described Valhalla:

All the men who have fallen in battle since the beginning of the world have now come to Odin in Valhalla. There is a huge crowd there, and there will be many more still, and yet they will seem too few when the wolf comes.

But there is never so big a crowd in Valhalla that they don't get enough pork from the boar called Sæhrímnir. He is boiled every day, and comes alive every evening.

Odin gives the food on his table to two wolves, but he himself needs nothing to eat. Wine is for him both food and drink. Two ravens sit on his shoulders and bring to his ears all the news that they see or hear. He sends them out at daybreak to fly over the whole world, and they come back at breakfast time; by this means he comes to know a great deal about what is going on, and on account of this men call him the god-of-ravens.

Every day after they have dressed, Odin's champions put on their armour and go out into the courtyard and fight and lay one another low. That is their play and, when it is breakfast time, they ride to the hall and sit down to drink.

There are, moreover, others whose duty it is to serve in Valhalla, carry the drinks round and look after the table service and ale cups. These are called Valkyries. Odin sends them to every battle and they choose death for the men destined to die, and award victory.

After the conversion of the King of Norway in 994, the Christian faith soon attracted a large number of adherents in Iceland. Pagans and Christians soon made up two groups of equal importance in the *Althing*. During the annual meeting of the parliament in the year 1000 news spread that a volcanic eruption had occurred at Reykjanes, which before the period of colonization, was the site of intensive volcanic activity. The pagan faction concluded that the gods were angry. "What angered the gods when the lava flowed which we now stand on?" asked one of the chieftains from the Christian side Snorri Goði, well known for his cleverness. The conflict between pagans and Christians hung in the balance, and the leader of the moderate pagans was charged with the task of finding a solution that would avert the worst. It is said that he spent three days running deep in thought under his sheepskin before emerging with the following compromise: all would adopt the new religion of Christianity, either through an oath of allegiance or through silence. Yet every Icelander would be free to make sacrifices, to maintain ancient rites and practise the ancestral religion so long as this was done privately and discreetly. Both sides were happy with the compromise and the pagans were allowed to continue eating horsemeat.

The Lutheran Reformation

The second act in Iceland's religious drama was played out in the sixteenth century at the time of the Reformation. Iceland had lost its independence and had passed under the control of the Norwegian crown in 1262. When their protector, itself ruled by Denmark, became Protestant in the 1530s, Icelanders were again instructed to change faith. The Catholic bishop Jón Arason, helped by his two sons (his interpretation of celibacy was apparently relaxed), organized resistance to what he saw as Danish cultural and religious imperialism. He enjoyed almost absolute power in Iceland, which he wielded in the name of a pope who was so far removed from everyday life as to be invisible. Yet he was captured in November 1550 after a fight known as the Battle of Sauðafell by a sheriff in the pay of the Danish authorities. When he was beheaded along with his two sons at Skálholt, in the words of the writer Thor Vilhjálmsson "the last standard bearer of national pride for several centuries died". Jón Arason remains an ambiguous figure, an autocrat who rebelled against a foreign authority, but paradoxically he is celebrated by today's Lutheran community as a hero—perhaps because he is the only figure in Icelandic history to have died for his convictions.

The execution of Jón Arason marked a turning point in the History of Iceland. After his death there was no obstacle to the Reformation, no impediment to the power of the king. The treasure and lands of the church and the monasteries were confiscated by the crown. Danish noblemen were put in charge of the administration. They resided in Denmark, usually visiting Iceland only in the summer. Penalties for many crimes were increased. The supreme court in Copenhagen became the highest court of appeal for the Icelanders, while the *Althing* lost its importance. In practice the country was treated like a Danish colony.

Arndís Jónsdóttir: Mother Courage

Rulings on moral issues became extraordinarily severe after the Reformation, with adultery and illegitimate births pitilessly punished. Historians tend to disagree as to how to interpret these laws, with nationalists blaming the Danes for imposing harsher legislation in their colony than in Denmark, and feminists pointing out that the Vikings and then Christians executed men and flagellated women but that after the Reformation women were condemned to death by drowning. Adulterous women or those pregnant outside wedlock were punished, but not men. The most recent research suggests that this legalized cruelty was simply an austerity measure, the aim of each bailiwick (the local court) being to reduce the number of women financially dependent on the local authority through a policy of sexual repression. It was forbidden, for instance, to take a pregnant, unmarried woman into one's house in case she gave birth and made the local community responsible for bringing up the child. Heavy punishments could also be a source of revenue for the administration as large fines could be paid in place of a prison term. The following episode—discovered in contemporary annals by the historian Inga Huld Hákonardóttir—took place at the end of the eighteenth century, when the moral laws were no longer applied with the same severity.

Arndís Jónsdóttir, often called barna-Arndís (Arndís-with-children) was born around 1745, the daughter of poor parents living at Gamla Hraun near Eyrarbakki in the south of Iceland. Her turbulent life began in Meðalland, near Skaftafell, where she was taken on at a very young age as a servant. There she soon gave birth to two children fathered by a married man (he denied paternity of the first but recognized the second) and was driven out of the canton and sent back to Eyrarbakki. There it soon became apparent that she was pregnant for a third time, the father being another farmer in the district where she was a servant. She was brought before the bailiff who, with the support of a jury of eight local farmers, issued the following verdict: "Arndís Jónsdóttir having admitted relations with married men is condemned in accordance with the *hórdómur* register of morality laws to be executed by drowning." The judgement was made in 1771, the first guilty verdict for adultery in a hundred years. The sentence was sent for approval that same summer to parliament, where men with more nuanced legal understanding pointed out that she was not married and perhaps was not aware that the fathers of her children were married. The judges finally ruled against her initial guilty verdict arguing that "it was impossible for a woman to have relations with men against their will especially if these men were married". She was finally ordered to pay a fine of twelve *aurar* (or forty metres of woollen cloth), but Arndís was insolvent and the judges changed the sentence to a prison term of four years. Terrible rumours surrounded the women's prison in Copenhagen—but Arndís was lucky. A new prison had just opened at Arnarhóll, now a district in Reykjavik housing the prime minister's office. Conditions, at least for the first years, were tolerable, the food was edible and the prisoners were relatively free as they performed various forms of hard labour for the inhabitants of what was then the minuscule village of Reykjavik. The prison was home to some colourful characters, one of them a vagabond named Arnes who counted among his friends some notorious outlaws. Arnes soon took a liking to her and she had two more children with him (whom he insouciantly disowned as not his).

These last two children were not added to the list for which Arndís had been jailed, and she was released and returned to her family in Eyrarbakki. Yet by now she was carrying another child and a few months later gave birth to her sixth child, the father this time, according to her, being a fisherman from the north whom she had met in Reykjavik and who had returned home. Luckily there was a new bailiff in her district and there was no risk of death by drowning; instead she was banished from living in the south of the country. At the age of thirty, she left her birthplace and went to Hafnarfjörður, to the south of Reykjavik, where she met Nikulás Bárðarson, married but separated from his wife. She had her seventh child with him and, despite the efforts of the priest to separate the couple, an eighth.

Again the local authorities called for her to be executed for infringing the morality laws and again a sort of luck was on her side in the summer of 1784 as instead she was condemned to life imprisonment in Copenhagen. As the prospect of spending the rest of her life with murderers and lunatics loomed, another option presented itself: to marry a man willing to take financial charge of the condemned woman. Men of this sort were rare but Arndís, who was always resourceful, managed to find one: Magnús Pálsson, a sixty-year-old widower from Reykjavik. He duly asked for her hand, but the poor man's health was already deteriorating and he died on 15 June 1785—at more or less the same moment that the royal authorization of the marriage arrived from Copenhagen.

Arndís was released, despite the death of her intended, and now, more mature, she opted for stability and married a certain Jón Jónsson, with whom she had a ninth child, the only legitimate one. Arndís died in 1803, aged sixty; she had given birth to nine children from at least six different men, single or married. She had twice been threatened with judicial drowning and narrowly avoided being sent to a certain death in the notorious women's prison.

Christian Faith and Popular Beliefs

Icelandic faith, although Lutheran and mostly austere, is strongly influenced by paganism and folk beliefs. The "fire priest" Jón Steingrímsson was in his church with his parishioners on 20 July 1783 when the Laki eruption suddenly doubled in intensity. The country was then living through the darkest period of its existence, with famines and epidemics following successive eruptions. Steingrímsson had recorded the hardships in his diary:

> This past week, and the two prior to it, more poison fell from the sky than words can describe: ash, volcanic hairs, rain full of sulphur and saltpeter, all of it mixed with sand. The snouts, nostrils, and feet of livestock grazing or walking on the grass turned bright yellow and raw. All water went tepid and light blue in color and gravel slides turned gray. All the earth's plants burned, withered and turned gray, one after another, as the fire increased and neared the settlements.

That day the renewed violence of the eruption threatened the small settlement of Kirkjubæjarklaustur, the church and those inside, as a molten lava stream approached rapidly. The priest began to pray among the din of falling rocks and sizzling lava, and his prayers were miraculously answered as the lava stream stopped some distance away from the church. It was a very Catholic miracle for a Lutheran priest, but Steingrímsson's "fire sermon" became celebrated throughout Iceland.

Apart from miracles, Icelanders are deeply interested in a range of phenomena that includes elves, trolls, ghosts and spirits. Scientific studies suggest that 72 per cent of Icelanders believe in spirits, 68 per cent in magic places and 55 per cent in elves. Such concepts find pride of place on Iceland's official coat-of-arms, where a dragon and a rock-giant stand as national tutelary protectors alongside a bull and a griffin. People also like to make claims regarding supernatural events and will tell the sceptical visitor that the course of a particular road was changed during construction so that elves would not be disturbed. Instructions were also given that the rocks next to the projected Harpa concert hall should be removed gently by the bulldozer because they contained the memories of supernatural beings. Whether people really believe in such phenomena is open to question, and it may be nearer the truth that they want other people to believe in them and so maintain this national idiosyncrasy. In any case, it seems unlikely that road builders spend too much time in negotiation with spirits.

In the event of an unexpected meeting with a supernatural being in fog or in the depths of the arctic winter it is useful to classify the different types so that no gaffe is made in addressing the creature in question. First come the ghosts or phantoms (*draugar*), living corpses who tend to talk noisily at night in wooden houses with creaking boards. They should not be confused with spirits (*fylgjur*), whose sub-species, *sendingar* or messengers, have magic powers and are sent to carry out acts of vengeance. These are often former ghosts who have been recycled against their own will to take the life of an enemy. As for the spirits, they were initially friendly enough but from the eighteenth century, when famines and poverty gave everyday life a tragic character, they turned themselves into harbingers of a malevolent fate. Next come the elves (*álfar*) who are generally invisible and live in parallel to humans in magic places (*álagablettir*) which can be large rocks, cairns or simply meadows. They are present mainly in folk tales or stories that can be traced back to a collective memory. Trolls (*troll*), finally, are giants who live in the mountains and move about at night—but they have to return to their mountain hiding-place by dawn or they are immediately turned to stone. This is a pleasing notion since we have only to look up to the cliffs and crags that surround Reykjavik to see the most picturesque and grotesque examples of those who failed to return in time.

The Last Troll

There is a rich children's literature located in the world of elves and trolls, while adults also enjoy ghost stories. An English illustrator Brian Pilkington created such a successful image of trolls in 1981 illustrating a story written by Guðrún Helgadóttir, that Icelanders can no longer imagine trolls in any other way.

Another story *Tryggðatröll* (*The Last Troll*), written by Steinar Berg is set in the Breiðafjörður bay, where mountains and rivers have played a huge part in the region's history, and begins in the world of humans. The farmer's wife Guðrún laments that she is unable to become pregnant. One day she falls asleep after gathering blueberries and dreams that a troll has told her that he will help her to realize her dream of having a child. She duly becomes pregnant and gives birth to Bergsteinn, a strong, healthy boy. Years later Bergsteinn, now an adult, is helping to gather in the sheep before winter when he becomes lost and is helped by the young female troll Drífa, who welcomes him into the shelter of her cave. For several years running he seeks her out during the autumn sheep gathering season and finally asks for her hand in marriage, brings her into the world of humans and sets up home with her in a new farm. They have a daughter Sumarrós, and when the priest comes to see the child he realizes that he is the father of Drífa because he, too, many years previously had stumbled into the parallel troll world.

At Christmas Bergsteinn and his daughter go to mass, while Drífa waits for them at home. On his way back Bergsteinn is caught in the treacherous ice of a river and dies saving Sumarrós. Again time passes and Sumarrós is married but with no children. Drífa lives with her daughter, but as trolls live much longer than humans she eventually sees Sumarrós die of old age. Believing that the time has now come to leave this existence, she asks a friendly fairy to help her pass back into the troll world and allows herself to be caught by the rising sun and turned into stone.

Churches in Crisis

The official National Church of Iceland has lost influence and prestige over recent years, with a system of priests spread among parishes no longer reflecting the reality of a country where migration from the countryside has irreversibly changed society. The institution remains resolutely traditional in outlook and has hardly been touched by the debates and controversies that have stirred up the churches in Scandinavia. But many oppose the separation of Church and state and among them some unlikely supporters from the ranks of the far left. They argue that small island communities, in particular Protestants, tend to split into divisive sects (the Faroe Islands are cited as an example). An official, state-endorsed Church, even moderately corrupt, would therefore be the best bulwark against the atomization of religious life and sectarian conflict.

The Catholic Church, in contrast, witnessed steady growth with an influx of foreign workers, notably from Poland and the Philippines (there are even two Polish priests who work exclusively with their compatriots), but since the crisis in 2008 many of these have returned home. Catholicism has long offered an alternative to the established Church, and the prominent author and Nobel Prize winner Halldór Laxness was a convert before he discovered socialism. But it was also a victim of a lack of religious tolerance and despite Danish pressure freedom to worship arrived as late as 1874. The Catholic chapel built for French fishermen was, as we have seen, off-limits to the people of Reykjavik, with one of the capital's two policemen stationed at the door.

All churches, but especially the Catholic Church, have been affected by the revelation in 2011 of paedophile abuse, and it has been alleged that the police failed to take action following numerous complaints and allegations. Even if rumours had been circulating for many years, the open accusations came as a major shock nationwide, with some calling, in vain, for the resignation of the head of the established Church.

Reykjavik's Churches

The Dómkirkjan and the 1881 parliament building in Reykjavik are among the oldest and perhaps the most beautiful buildings in Iceland. The Dómkirkjan is formally the cathedral of the National Church of Iceland but it is the much larger Hallgrímskirkja that hosts important ceremonies. The neoclassical Dómkirkjan may not be entirely harmonious in its design and proportions—the copper lining at the base of the tower, built later, is strangely dimensioned— but it is precisely these eccentricities that account for its beauty and originality just as its modest size contrasts with the importance of its function.

The church is testimony to the blunderings of the Danish colonial period. After the bishop had moved from Skálholt to Reykjavik in 1785 the building of a church became a priority, the one in Aðalstræti being minuscule. The stone was quarried in nearby Grjótaþorp, and winter was awaited so that they could be transported on sledges. Builders in Denmark were sent for the following year, but according to legend they were often drunk and made a mess of the roof, which had to be rebuilt in 1792, a few months after work was finished. When the church was finally inaugurated it could hold all of Reykjavik's worshippers but almost at once it began to leak, the beams being rotten. Specialists sent from Denmark—again it was considered by the colonial power that Icelanders were incapable of doing the job—inspected the building and recommended that services be stopped until a third roof was built, which happened two years later. Even then the regular church-goers were fearful, and when a beam began to groan loudly during a service the congregation rushed to the door, some were forced to break windows and jump to safety by the panicked crowd blocking the exit.

The Dómkirkjan was rebuilt and enlarged in the mid-nineteenth century, again by Danish craftsmen. At the time the church also accommodated the national library, the museum of natural history and the archives—a far cry from today's uncluttered and unadorned interior. Incompetence struck again in the twentieth century when large-scale renovations were undertaken with inappropriate building materials, leading to further alterations within a few years.

A group of some 600 parishioners split from the official Church in 1899 to found a Free Church parish (*Fríkirkjusöfnuður*) and as this Lutheran congregation grew in size its church building, the Fríkirkjan, was enlarged and consecrated on three occasions. Sited on the edge of Tjörnin, this simple and modest white church with its distinctive tower and green roof is wooden but entirely clad in corrugated iron. Plain and unadorned, the exterior reveals that the corrugated iron has been cut to allow windows but without wooden frames. The oldest parts date to 1903.

Hallgrímskirkja is Reykjavik's biggest church and an unmissable landmark standing on the hill at Þingholt overlooking the city. Built on land occupied during the Second World War by military barracks, work started almost immediately after the war, based on plans commissioned in 1937 from state architect Guðjón Samúelsson and continued into the 1980s and 1990s, with a major restoration undertaken in 1999. The distinctive form of the concrete church is widely considered to be influenced by Icelandic geology and landscape, the massive tower alluding to the country's spectacular basalt columns and traces of lava flows. The interior houses a magnificent organ, the only conspicuous feature in a starkly plain interior dominated by soaring columns, which has over 5,000 pipes and a case measuring over fifty feet in height. The church's acoustics, however, have been criticized, and many have also been unflattering in their reaction to the building itself and its allegedly phallic steeple.

Most Icelanders, conversely, approve of the neo-gothic concrete Catholic cathedral at Landakot in western Reykjavik, built on the site of the former French chapel by the same architect, Guðjón Samúelsson, and completed in 1929—although readers from nations with longer traditions may not agree. The Landakotskirkja nevertheless has an interesting history that can be traced back to Denmark's insistence that Iceland allow religious freedom and pluralism. It was then that it was decided to replace the wooden chapel with a church worthy of the name, a relatively (in comparison with Hallgrímskirkja) conventional design with a flat-topped, square tower. The Lutheran municipal authorities did their best to obstruct the ambitions of the Catholic minority—in much the same way as problems have more recently surrounded a proposed mosque—but the church was eventually completed and before the advent of Hallgrímskirkja was the capital's largest place of worship.

The country's best churches are perhaps to be seen outside Reykjavik. Generally built on raised ground and surrounded by a cemetery, they are constructed of wood and often roofed with corrugated iron. With their whitewashed walls and red painted roofs, they are often charmingly simple, but they are also often too small to accommodate all those invited to a wedding and, more particularly, a funeral. Those who cannot find a seat inside are given an order of service and the radio wavelength on which the ceremony is to be transmitted. After listening in their cars to a "drive-in" service, they can then join the mourners for the burial ceremony and the inevitable drinks afterwards.

Visitors to the western fjords can see the extraordinary little wooden chapel on Papey Island, a place so windy (160 mph during a storm in October 2012), that the tiny church is securely fastened to the ground by a heavy chain. Popular legend has it that churches have been known to fly heavenwards in Iceland—in a mix of extreme climatic conditions and religious enthusiasm.

The Pagan Community

All Icelanders are obliged to pay a church tax, and the overwhelming majority (ninety per cent plus) pay it to the Lutheran National Church of Iceland. All recognized religions are eligible for contributions from their members, and atheists have to pay their tax to the secular University of Iceland. A certain number of non-Christians, however, prefer to make their payments to the neo-pagan Ásatrúarfélag, which has almost two thousand members of whom a third are women. For some the attraction lies in the group's attachment to folkloric Nordic pantheism and ancient gods, while for others it is little more than an amusing hoax (or in some cases a pretext for pagan-style feasting). Like any priest from the National Church of Iceland, high priests are legally entitled to officiate at marriage ceremonies.

The high priest Sveinbjörn Beinteinsson (1924-93) was for a long time an emblematic figure in the pagan community. A farmer and poet, he was often seen with his huge white beard on the streets of Reykjavik—an eccentric of the sort much beloved by Icelanders. He was—surprisingly for a follower of Odin and Thor—buried according to Lutheran rites, but he may in the end have hedged his bets. His stone monument stands on the hill at Öskjuhlíð near the Perlan installations and it provides members of the pagan church with a place to conduct sacrifices—of a symbolic nature, of course.

9

Changing Faces
Migration and Social Change

Iceland, unlike Scandinavian countries where xenophobia is nowadays relatively common, does not have a racist political party. This is partly because the country has not experienced a significant influx of foreigners with its political ramifications and partly because populism in Iceland has taken other forms such as the nationalist refusal to pay Icesave's debts to Britain and the Netherlands and support for mavericks such as Jón Gnarr and his Best Party, which has promised a cocaine-free parliament in Reykjavik by 2020 and free towels at swimming pools.

There are various reasons for Icelandic racial tolerance. To begin with, most Icelanders consider themselves both foreigners and separate from their Scandinavian cousins. How, it is asked, did they find the strength to fight for the nation's independence when they had the same culture, the same religion and originally the same language as their colonial masters? Insularity served as a way of explaining the difference between Iceland and the rest of Scandinavia, especially when the island in question was hundreds of miles away from its closest neighbours. An ethnic basis for this difference was then discovered in the idea of a supposedly Celtic identity, which is likely to be more imaginary than real. The Vikings, so this theory went, collected shiploads of Celtic slaves from Ireland and the Scottish islands who were brought to Iceland. That is why, according to some, Icelanders are poetic, ill-disciplined and fond of partying, while Scandinavians are organized, puritanical and mean. If it is true that the Celts left a few words in Icelandic and that Irish monks lived in Iceland before the Vikings, it is still a far cry from a cultural melting-pot, and it has been suggested that the slaves were in fact other Vikings who had lost their freedom through gambling. What is significant is not so much ethnic characteristics, even if some are

African drummers (courtesy Visit Reykjavik)

obsessed with blood groups and skull shapes, but pride in a Celtic heritage within Icelandic collective memory.

The saying that Icelanders are strangers in their own island does not only refer to the colonization of the ninth century but goes back even further. Iceland was not a destination for the Vikings but a staging-post. It was a place where there was endless grazing for their animals, 240 species of birds and fish for times of famine. It was also a place where the climate was not too harsh, and above all there was plenty of empty land. But it was also a snare, and despite a few incursions westwards to North America the Vikings stayed. And though they stayed they never lived "in harmony" with their environment. There is no evidence before the twentieth century of traditions or customs connected with the cold, of architectural solutions to deal with the wind. People who live in harmony with their environment tend to excel in the decorative arts, but Icelanders, who have always had to struggle against theirs, prefer to seek refuge in fiction, a means of escaping the rigours of everyday life. They have long been at home among books, works of art and musical performances, but anything that is not culture with a capital c—interior decoration, gastronomy, gardening—has only recently aroused their interest. Foreigners, perhaps naively and because they have come to admire the loneliness and the majestic calm of the frozen wastes, expect Icelanders to live in harmony with their landscape. But, in truth, few can live in harmony with a landscape that is covered in snow half the year, where nothing happens and where making a living or having fun are impossible. Icelanders are the descendants of itinerant farmers who settled on the island because the grass was green, who stayed when the climate deteriorated and who set about fishing for other people when those people stopped fishing in their own waters.

An island is always a place from where people migrate, and island dwellers are accustomed to having children and seeing them leave. Everybody has a family member living abroad. In short, there are more Icelanders overseas than foreigners living in Iceland—and for that reason it is hard to resent somebody arriving from elsewhere when one is ready and willing to leave. Icelanders generally assume that those who leave will return, perhaps because they only see those again who have come home. Others disappear until the time when their curious grandchildren come to meet their little cousins, but by then the unifying bonds of language are already broken.

Foreigners in Iceland

After centuries when the only foreigners whom Icelanders saw were Danish traders and occasional European fishermen, the arrival of a US military base at Keflavik, only 25 miles from the capital, was a shock. The Americans were rich, and local girls hid inside the boots of cars to be smuggled into dances at the base. The Icelandic authorities reputedly asked the US military to stop sending black troops after several girls became pregnant, and the American army agreed and kept its promise until the beginning of the 1970s. In fact, the Icelandic request was more subtle, the Americans being asked to deploy only one or two black servicemen "so that Icelanders could gradually get used to them". The troops led a strange, segregated existence in their base, situated on the windiest part of Iceland. Only married troops were allowed to venture into Reykjavik once a week on Wednesday, the day that alcohol was forbidden in restaurants.

In the fish processing industry, however, Iceland needed foreign labour to de-scale, decapitate, skin, de-worm and generally beautify the cod destined for British fish and chip shops. The selection of workers in the 1970s and 1980s was made on ethnic grounds, and as Britain was already a multiracial society the Icelandic fishing companies preferred to recruit in London but among the Australian, New Zealand and South African communities, where young white women were the preferred employees. They had usually hoped—and failed—to find a job in Britain and came to work for several months. An English author wrote a very funny piece on their lives whose Icelandic title "Ísaðar gellur" means both "cods' cheeks on ice" and "drunken girls".

Nowadays fish factory workers are from Poland or Asia, notably the Philippines and Thailand. The industry is now male-dominated, both in the onshore factories and on the trawlers which have increasingly become factory ships. In some cases young Thai women have married older Icelandic fishermen, whose long expeditions did not equip them to keep pace with Icelandic women's growing emancipation and who console themselves over their broken marriages with Asian girlfriends whom they believe—fortunately wrongly—to be more docile. Most Poles are married and are scattered among Iceland's village communities. Those from the Baltic States generally work in the construction sector but many have left since the 2008 crash. The departure of foreign workers hastened the crisis in the property market, but few locals rushed to fill the jobs they left behind. Only a significant growth in the Asian community has made up for the departure of European migrants.

Otherness and Language

Icelanders' nearest neighbours are the inhabitants of Greenland. They are less than 300 kilometres from the Icelandic coast but seem much further away than the British or the Norwegians who are, in fact, even more distant. They are called *Grænlendingar* or Greenlanders and rarely *Inúítar* or Inuits. (Icelanders become terribly annoyed when a foreigner asks if there are Eskimos in Iceland.)

The Icelandic language classifies countries and peoples into three categories. Some have the honour of a unique name: the English are *Bretar*, the Scottish *Skotar* and the Irish *Írar*. Certain cities are "translated" into Icelandic, such as *Lundúnir* (London) or *Jórvík* (York). The French are *Frakkar*, natives perhaps of *Rúðuborg* (Rouen), and Germans are *Þjóðverjar*. In the second group are –*menn* (men) like *Kanadamenn* (Canadians), *Brasilíumenn* (Brazilians) and *Austurríkismenn* (Austrians). Even further removed are those in the third category, who are more modestly *búar* (inhabitants): hence *Marokkóbúar* (Moroccans), *Senegalbúar* (Senegalese) or *Malíbúar* (Malians).

Icelanders as Seen by Foreign Visitors

W. H. Auden's first trip to Iceland in 1936 inspired his *Letters from Iceland*, a mixture of poems, travel stories, quotations from other writers and snippets of advice. In Chapter 6, "Sheaves from Sagaland", he humorously recounts the experiences and perceptions

of his predecessors, eighteenth- and nineteenth-century travellers such as W. G. Collingwood, an academic and artist specializing in the sagas, and Niels Horrebow, a Danish natural historian.
What does Iceland look like?

"The map of Iceland has been sometimes drawn by schoolboys as an eider duck, quacking with wide-opened beak." (W. G. Collingwood)

Concerning the capital:
"Reykjavik is, unquestionably, the worst place in which to spend the winter in Iceland. The tone of the society is the lowest that can well be imagined . . . It not only presents a lamentable blank to the view of the religious observer, but is totally devoid of every source of intellectual gratification." (Ebenezer Henderson)

The immortal bard proves that nothing escapes him:
"Pish for me, Iceland dog. Thou prick-eared cur of Iceland." (Shakespeare, *Henry IV*)

The Icelanders are human:
"They are not so robust and hardy that nothing can hurt them; for they are human beings and experience the sensations common to mankind." (Niels Horrebow)

Concerning their eyes:
"A very characteristic feature of the race is the eye, dure and cold as a pebble—the mesmerist would despair at the first sight." (Sir Richard Burton)

Concerning their mouth:
"The oral region is often coarse and unpleasant." (Sir Richard Burton)

Concerning their habits:
"If I attempted to describe some of their nauseous habits, I might fill volumes."
(Ida Pfeiffer)

Concerning their kissing:
"I have sometimes fancied, when they took their faces apart, that I could hear a slight clicking sound; but this might be imagination." (Frederick Howell)

Concerning their music:
"I heard a voice in the farm singing an Icelandic song. At distance it resembled the humming of bees." (Ida Pfeiffer)

Concerning their dancing:
"They have no idea of dancing, though the merchants at the factories for their diversion will get a fiddle and make them dance, in which they succeed no better than by hopping and jumping about." (Niels Horrebow)

Concerning their lack of education:
"It is not uncommon in Iceland for people of all ranks, ages and sexes to sleep in the same apartment. Their notions of decency are unavoidably not very refined; but we had sufficient proof that the instances of this which we witnessed proceeded from ignorance, and expressed nothing but perfect ignorance." (Sir George Steuart McKenzie)

What is striking about these quotations is not so much their negativity—this is a selection chosen to make a point—but the distance that the foreign observers put between themselves and the people they are describing, a people both European and Christian. Little wonder perhaps that Icelanders have long been susceptible to an inferiority complex when confronted with scrutiny from abroad.

On the Move
Icelanders are always on the move, willing to live and work abroad—and this does not only apply to those with sought-after skills. An Icelander may be unwilling to work as a road sweeper in Iceland but will not see doing the same job in Denmark as degrading. This willingness to move goes back into the mists of time; the Vikings

always tried their luck elsewhere, while farmers from past centuries were always in search of new land, new horizons. Today it is Norway that exerts an attraction for its high salaries, and Denmark (whose language all schoolchildren have learnt) for its pleasant lifestyle, and there are nurses, for instance, who split their time each month between Iceland and Norway to earn two wages. The country's collective memory abounds in stories of Icelanders returning home with their fortune made, but nowadays it is more likely to be a case of young people leaving and disappearing from the same collective memory. The present author lost the service of his 84-year-old plumber (people work to an old age) when he left to join his daughter who had long since emigrated to Australia.

At the end of the nineteenth century between twelve and fifteen per cent of Iceland's population set sail for the northern United States and the Manitoba region of Canada. In the twentieth they moved to Scandinavia and Australia when herring stocks collapsed in 1967 and unemployment appeared. Some 3,500 Icelandic women married and followed American troops back to the United States, and many graduates educated there stayed to find work. There are now thousands of Icelanders in Copenhagen, Oslo and Stockholm, and there are more people of Icelandic origin around the world than in Iceland itself.

The Canadian Eldorado

In Kinmount, Ontario, about a hundred kilometres from Toronto, a statue by the railway station commemorates the Icelanders who laid the rails almost a century and a half ago. The railway line no longer exists, the station is closed and there are no more Icelanders in Kinmount.

In the poverty-stricken Iceland of 1875 people dreamt of migrating, not to America as in the 1950s or the Norway of 2010, but to Canada. About 350 of them combined together to pay for their journey, but the merchant in charge cheated them and they had to find another way, finally disembarking at Quebec and moving on to Toronto. There they heard that labour was needed in the building of a railway line, and with women and children the

Icelandic migrants headed for Kinmount. The shantytown huts where they lived were unheated, and thirty of them died in the first two years, including twenty-six children who were buried in the woods in graves that have never been found. This was not the end of their tribulations; the company building the railway line then went bust. The Canadian authorities finally became concerned with their fate, not least because the British Governor of Ontario knew and admired Iceland. The survivors were moved to Gimli, near Lake Winnipeg, where land was distributed free-of-charge in a settlement that was called "New Iceland".

It might have been assumed that the colonists, originating from a cold climate, would have adapted to the rigours of the Canadian winter, but this was not the case. They had wanted from the outset to settle by the sea as they knew how to fish and thought that the nearby lakes would offer the same opportunities, yet they had no experience of fishing on frozen lakes and knew little about hunting small game. The first years were dreadful, before they began to adapt, and as they were Icelanders they wrote a great deal about their experiences. Among the many sources that chart their existence was a newspaper, *Heimskringla*, written in Icelandic. The language was passed down to the second generation, and in part to the third, then it began to disappear. The paper appeared half in English in the years after the Second World War, and Iceland sent a journalist to edit the Icelandic part. Eventually the newspaper, amalgamated in 1959 with the *Lögberg* to become the *Lögberg Heimskringla*, was published entirely in English. In this sense, the history of Vinland lived on, and links between Iceland and the so-called *Vestur-Íslendingar*, the Icelanders of the West, remain strong.

The Jews of Iceland

The Danish merchants who came to settle in Iceland were often of Jewish descent, and Danish law restricted their access to property. In 1913 Fritz Heymann Nathan formed a company in Reykjavik and was responsible for one of the capital's multi-storey office buildings lit by electric lights. Yet the Jewish community was not defined by ethnic identity or religious practices, and the first Jewish ceremony took place during the Second World War when Jewish servicemen in the British military were present. Two Icelandic prime ministers were descendants of the Danish merchants but little attention was drawn to their origins. In his journal William Morris mentioned a certain Zoëga, who arranged horses for his party and was descended from an Italian Jew who had sought refuge in Denmark in the sixteenth century after killing a man in a duel. Morris recalled him as "a big fellow, red-haired, blue-eyed and long-legged, like a Scotch gardener". Some Jewish musicians came to Iceland before the Second World War escaping Nazism and played an important role in the development of music in the country.

An Egalitarian Society?

Many visitors to Iceland, even before arriving, are convinced that they are about to witness the inner workings of an egalitarian society. The British are impressed that Icelanders address each other by their first name, the French by the absence of the formal *vous*, Germans by the fact that names are never associated with titles. Americans enjoy being able to walk around the city centre in safety, the Dutch having access to so much space and the Irish the fact that everybody speaks the same language, carefully preserved unlike Gaelic. Southern Europeans admire the gender equality and are impressed that only three years separate male and female life expectancy. All these visitors confess their admiration to the Icelanders they meet, who in turn confirm that their society is indeed extremely egalitarian. It is certainly a pleasure to hear such a flattering account of themselves, especially after they have spent all day cursing the government, corruption, nepotism, the huge debt . . . and growing inequality.

Before the collapse of the economy there was a kind of official discourse that everybody subscribed to, a code of good behaviour that all—except those who had left Iceland—respected. It stated, in short, that Iceland had kept its innocence, that the island had never been at war, that it had no enemies who bore a grudge. The bank crash, of course, put an end to that. But the idea remained that "small is beautiful", and it is true that the small population does create the conditions for a greater degree of equality than in other, bigger societies. An Icelander is more likely to be able to say that his cousin is a friend of the prime minister than an Englishman claiming that his cousin knows the Royal Family. Software exists in Iceland, managed by the human genetic research company deCODE, that allows the user with a single click on his name and that of anyone else to find any family links. People, however important, are called by their first name, and all individuals in the telephone directory are also listed by first name.

If someone is appointed to a prestigious job, the news appears in the newspapers and is discussed during the coffee break in every office. One person will know the lucky man's wife, another will have been in the same class at school, and perhaps someone's children know his children. Such familiarity would be unthinkable in a society numbering tens of millions of inhabitants. Ties of friendship are tight; attempts to open "exclusive" nightclubs have always failed as everybody is used to going to the same bars, discotheques and nightclubs. What is true in a provincial town abroad applies here to a capital city.

All Icelanders speak the same language as there are not enough of them for dialects or slang linked to a region or a social group to exist. Only young people use words and phrases that belong to them alone until their parents adopt them and they then drop them and invent others. Fashions in clothing are more homogeneous than elsewhere, as are tastes in interior decoration. Icelanders go to see the same plays in the theatre and read the same books at Christmas (or at least buy the same books). Only the choice of where to go abroad on holiday, however, is a real social signifier.

Yet within a population of only 320,000 discrepancies in wealth exist in spectacular form. The country's richest man in 2008, Björgólfur Thor Björgólfsson, had a fortune that *Forbes* magazine estimated to be worth a third of Iceland's annual national budget. If initially the wealth of the super-rich was a cause of national pride—it had, after all, been made abroad and not by exploiting fellow countrymen—public opinion changed when the oligarchs started building their sumptuous residences, generally away from Reykjavik in the counrtyside. These palaces inspired envy and offended the sensibilities of the less conspicuously rich.

No district in Reykjavik can be said to be a symbol of social exclusion, but within each district there are clear social gradations. Whether in Kópavogur, Grafarvogur or Breiðholt, the same hierarchy applies: apartments, terraced houses and detached dwellings in rising value and status. The social mix is perhaps greatest in the centre of town, the most sought-after area, because here the poorest (or the youngest) often live in the basement or attic of a prosperous home.

As for the same language that everybody speaks, the limits of egalitarianism are to be found in the way in which a few sentences will betray the speaker's social origins, however tenuously. Anybody who enters a bus will be scrutinized—like anywhere else—for the giveaway indicators of social class: appearance, weight, behaviour. Prejudices apply as elsewhere—and using the bus is already a bad sign. And to return to the fortunate recipient of the prestigious post mentioned above, there is another, more cynical view of the process. Everybody knows the individual in question, and so, of course, does the committee that made the appointment. Who knows whether their choice was fair or fixed?

Equality and Diversity

Egalitarianism aside, Icelandic society has long been dominated by consensus, by the idea that in a small society everyone must aspire to the same goals at the same time. What is often and simplistically described as a tradition of consensus seems, when viewed from outside, rather charming. Viewed from the inside, however, this same tradition carries the weight of provincialism, the constraints of the extended family, and the burden of ingrained social habits and prohibitions (those concerning beer and dogs were only lifted in Reykjavik at the end of the 1980s).

The opening of the country to Europe and many forms of deregulation have liberated Icelanders from many of the constraints they faced in terms of social behaviour, dress, diet and so on. A libertarian ideology accompanied this process, and for a while one was either left-wing and nationalist—that is to say conservative in relation to lifting the prohibitions—or right-wing and libertarian, in other words in favour of ending restrictions. The end of social cohesion seemed a small price to pay for what was gained; the standard of living rose, the state of the roads improved, and Icelanders also freed themselves from the constraints of space—working fifty kilometres from home, spending a weekend in the north of the country or escaping on a break to Europe were now in the realm of the possible.

The multiple deregulations led to a noticeable rise in social inequalities. Many trade union rights were scrapped, and few young people wanted in any case to do manual jobs, as foreign workers were brought in to replace locals in the least desirable forms of work. It hardly seemed to matter as everyone, whatever their status, was upwardly mobile. But this was not enough and from 2000 onwards a collective megalomania, utterly at odds with old constraints, took hold of a large part of the population. The banks realized that people now wanted jeeps and extra-large homes and responded by offering mortgages with no deposit and loans for cars at "advantageous" rates.

At the height of the boom between 2005 and 2008, the issue of inequality—as viewed from Iceland—was the old-fashioned preoccupation of an anaemic Europe. "You ain't seen nothing yet," claimed President Ólafur Ragnar Grímsson on a visit to London in 2005, boasting that "daring Icelandic entrepreneurs are succeeding where others hesitate or fail". The electorate continued to vote left or right through habit, atavism or conviction, but most voters irrespective of party were intoxicated by easy money and credit. In any case both Social Democrats and Conservatives governed together, taking turns singing the praises of the "Icelandic miracle" abroad, the financial phenomenon validated by triple-A ratings and promoted by the manoeuvres of unscrupulous entrepreneurs.

The awakening was cruel when everything collapsed, and the angry mob suddenly rediscovered its egalitarian reflexes. The bankrupt businessmen had to hide abroad or behind the darkened windows of their luxury jeeps. The left back in power tried to restore its radical credentials with a gay prime minister and talk of joining the European Union, in defiance of nationalist instincts.

Yet nostalgia for the good old days of ostentatious consumption has quickly surfaced. If the desire for transparency, the need to punish the guilty and the urge to build a fairer society are accompanied by rising unemployment, hardship, squeezed household budgets and chronic debt, it is not surprising that people feel drawn to the past. Isn't a state of prosperous corruption, it is whispered, better than an honest dog's life?

10 | **Consuming Interests**
Money and the Economy

Visitors to Reykjavik are often advised to do their shopping in Kringlan or Smáralind, the capital's two new out-of-town shopping centres. A trip here might be interesting sociologically but unless the weather is truly terrible there is not much point in spending time in places full of international chains. Everything that a visitor might want to buy—from supermarket supplies to knitwear and the ubiquitous puffin memorabilia—is in any case available in the town centre, and the competition is such that bargains are to be had. The big malls are covered and air-conditioned replicas of Oxford Street, filled with alluring, even luxury consumer goods, and the suburbs in which they stand, with their recently repainted houses and latest model Range Rovers (at least until 2008) give an impression of opulence.

Yet despite this impression hourly wage rates are relatively weak by European standards, and it is by no means obvious how Icelanders manage to enjoy such a conspicuously high standard of living. One explanation is the amount of overtime worked, but this has been less the case since the economic crisis took hold. Another, more important factor is their spectacular indebtedness, double the average level of European Union countries in relation to the standard of living.

Why, outsiders ask, is there this long-established desire to live on credit? The Vikings were obsessed with gambling, to such an extent that modern historians believe that some of the slaves brought to Iceland by the early settlers were probably fellow Vikings who had forfeited their freedom through gambling losses. There has long been a culture of spending, of living for the moment; Icelanders have never been great hoarders.

For centuries the Danes held a monopoly over trade, and the small profits to be made from selling dried fish (stockfish) just about enabled households to buy basic necessities. Iceland produced no

Laugavegur, Reykjavik's main shopping street
(Tupungato/Wikimedia Commons)

salt, and the commercialization of salted fish only began in the nineteenth century. Today's collective image of the period before then is one of farmers making their way once a year to the town to sell their dried fish or wool. There the farmer might linger in Reykjavik—then no larger than a village—drink more than was sensible and eventually return home having spent a dangerous amount of the proceeds. The alcohol fumes that accompanied the repentant farmer were known as "the smell of the town", and whether or not this image is historically accurate it is one that Icelanders like to have of themselves: a carefree people, spendthrift and unconcerned with the future.

Mass consumerism dates from after the Second World War and in Iceland it took a form unknown elsewhere—perhaps because Icelanders are essentially a nation of fishermen. Those who make their money from fishing behave very differently from those who live from agriculture. Farming is vulnerable to unpredictable and damaging weather but it also requires consistency, regular hard work and a respect for the changing seasons. In fishing, however, luck plays a large part, and there are huge variations in the amount and value of the catch, sometimes leaving the fishing crew with a large and unforeseen income. The overwhelming temptation was always to spend the windfall at once and in one fell swoop—all the more so because life at sea is very hard. The fisherman has two lives, one at sea and the other on land which he had dreamt about while on the trawler, and the idea of saving money is largely alien. There will always be more fish to be caught and sold on the next expedition, and so everything that has been earned is to be spent and what is not yet earned can be borrowed from the bank. There is one unbreakable taboo in Iceland: drinking is never allowed on board a fishing boat. But many fishermen make up for lost time when back on shore, and the IKEA sitting room suite that was bought six months ago but smashed to pieces on the first drunken night back home will be replaced on credit and chosen by the wife—it is the least he can do for her. The prospect of paying back the loan by gutting cod on the deck as the seagulls swoop and squawk gives the fisherman a raison d'être, a sense of purpose.

Demography

The birth rate in Iceland, which was historically very high, also played its part, as those with several children were rarely in a position to save. A dynamic birth rate had several impacts on consumption: a large family must buy the goods necessary for its growth (household goods, bedding etc.); young adults, who make up a large part of the population, tend to consume more freely than older people; a sense of optimism pervades a young population, at least in a relatively wealthy western society where births are planned, who are keen to spend.

The baby boom generations acquired new homes, took on debts and were forced to buy more consumer goods as economic growth and consumption increased inexorably. Yet Iceland's demographic expansion was not to maintain the same pace as the period between 1955 and 1965 when it was that of a developing nation. The reasons for this dramatic spurt were various: the sparse population density (less than two inhabitants per square kilometre) in a still largely unsettled country; the ban on abortion which was only allowed later; and the positivity and desire to build a new nation that accompanied independence in 1944 and which was the main factor in demographic growth.

In the ensuing decade between 1965 and 1975 the birth rate dropped to an average of about three children per woman, a drop of about 25 per cent on the preceding period even if there were many mothers aged under twenty and births outside of marriage, nowadays commonplace across Europe, were widespread in Iceland. This had a demographic impact as young mothers who later formed stable relationships often added a further two or three children.

Since 1975 the birth rate has fallen slightly to just under two children per woman, a fact that is little known in Iceland where official discourse persists in praising a strong birth rate as the "undeniable" sign of health—a phenomenon at odds with the facts.

Inflation and Credit

Inflation, very high in Iceland since independence and long described as endemic, was a major factor in the country's hyper-consumption.

The war years saw the economy overheat as the British military presence, followed by that of the Americans, stimulated growth and spending as goods and tastes arrived from the United States. In the immediate post-war years inflation fell and the departure of the military produced a mini-recession, a process that was reversed with the return of the Americans and the creation of the NATO base at Keflavik as well as the advent of fish freezing which caused a boom and renewed inflation.

While similar to that experienced in continental Europe in the 1950s, inflation reached double digits in the 1960s as a policy of massive investment overheated the economy along with substantial increases in salaries. The sudden depletion of herring stocks in the north created a mini-recession but inflation returned with a vengeance in the 1970s, frequently topping 50 per cent annually. During this period it was not unusual to see a tin of peas with three price stickers on top of one another as shopkeepers' prices kept pace with inflation. Foreign exchange was severely restricted, and Icelanders on holiday were allowed to exchange only a meagre sum into foreign currency, with a twelve per cent tax on top. Inflation reached its climax in 1984 (84 per cent) and was only briefly halted between 1986 and 1987 with a dramatic decline in cod catches.

A sharp break with inflationary policy occurred in 1992 when long-time President and then Finance Minister Ólafur Ragnar Grímsson introduced special legislation to renege on a teachers' pay rise and to introduce a wage freeze with the support of unions and employers. There followed a period of relative price stability, even if inflationary tendencies have not entirely disappeared—but these have historically been counterbalanced by the pre-crisis strength of the Icelandic *króna* against other currencies. The 2008 banking crash and the ensuing devaluation of the *króna* (by 50 per cent over two years) had a devastating effect on Icelanders' standard of living, however, and created another sort of inflation as imported goods suddenly became extremely expensive as family incomes fell—and this before the salary cuts that were to follow.

Inflation, with the resulting fear of rising prices and lack of confidence in the national currency, has always pushed Icelanders into consuming, believing that savings will be eroded and that goods bought tomorrow will inevitably be dearer than today. This ingrained attitude has meant that they continued to adopt the same spendthrift behaviour even during periods of low inflation.

For centuries Iceland's cultural model was Denmark, with institutions, the social system, architecture and cuisine all copied from the colonial power. Britain was also a reference point, even before the arrival of British troops at the beginning of the Second World War. The imitation of the "American way of life", much remarked upon by visitors in the 1950s and 1960s, has almost disappeared, with only US jeeps and La-Z-Boy reclining chairs surviving. The days when the only television set to be found was at the US base at Keflavik are long gone—and McDonalds, symbol of the recent crisis, closed in 2009.

Yet even if Iceland has broken away from imitating US tastes and habits, the country's reliance on credit as a vehicle of consumerism places it within the same economic model. Within the European context, where countries are roughly divided between those that save and those that spend on credit, Iceland finds itself in the latter camp, made up principally of Protestant nations. In what appears a paradox Lutheran Icelanders are not generally moved by a Protestant work ethic and conscience to clear their debts—while the idea that southern Catholic nations happily indebt themselves is a fallacy.

Spending Power

According to the Icelandic Statistical Bureau (Hagstofa), Icelanders spend only 4.3 per cent of their disposable income on clothing—but this is a partial view of household spending as much clothing is bought abroad. The amount spent on housing is also relatively modest (20 per cent in 2007), particularly as this includes water, electricity and heating. The size and often luxurious appearance of many houses, especially in Reykjavik, might suggest that accommodation accounts for a large part of family budgets, but land is cheap in a country where space is not at a premium and the lack of snobbery concerning city-centre housing means that—unlike in the rest of Europe—property is no dearer in the centre of Reykjavik than in the suburbs. Most building work is carried out by construction companies, but the owner, sometimes helped by professionals, normally adds the finishing touches, reducing the overall cost of a new house. Finally, as a result of the conservative Independence Party's policies, Iceland is a country of homeowners (85 per cent), in contrast to Scandinavia where renting is much more common. While in Europe the percentage of homeowners is inversely proportional to per capita Gross Domestic Product, prosperous Iceland ranks in home ownership along with impoverished Greece. Buying apartments for letting is not widespread, and renting is relatively inexpensive even if the market is small and unregulated. The proportion of household expenditure devoted to transportation, however, is a high 16 per cent.

In the year of the crash 406,000 out of 879,000 recorded departures from the country were those of Icelanders, and even taking into account a small number leaving by boat this represents an average annual per capita 1.3 trips abroad. Going abroad is in itself an exercise in hyper-consumption, with most trips organized by group rather than individual and more often than not to Spain. The atmosphere is usually festive, enhanced by drinking and by the freedom of anonymity. These trips or journeys to sunnier climes are what people dream of during the long winter nights but are also the butt of jokes and mockery. Icelanders are estimated to spend 11.9 per cent of their income abroad, not including transportation. Part of this spending (computers, cameras etc.) takes place in dollars in the duty-free shops at Keflavik airport, but the overall amount spent abroad remains remarkably high. This figure puts the impact of foreign tourism within Iceland into context and challenges the view of those who see it as the country's saviour. Tourist expenditure in 2008 was calculated at 6.9 per cent of overall spending, meaning that foreigners in Iceland spent 57.9 per cent of the amount spent by Icelanders abroad. In 2007, before the crisis dampened what locals call the "joy of spending" (*kaupgleði*), foreign tourist spending in Iceland only accounted for 36 per cent of what Icelanders spent overseas. The huge increase of foreign tourists after 2011 may though have partly changed these figures.

Icelanders like shopping abroad because it is cheaper (the domestic market is small and transportation costs high), because there is more choice but also because they see it as a hard-fought for right dating back to the time when their foreign exchange allowance was so tightly controlled. Since 2010 they have been allowed to take 300,000 *krónur* ($2,300) rather than 500,000 *krónur* ($3,800) but they can still use their credit cards, even if the limit was reduced for everybody after 2009.

Christmas shopping, until the events of 2008, was very much a foreign affair, with overseas weekend shopping sprees taking place in November—as it was considered improper to celebrate the bacchanals of consumerism during the period of Advent. Dublin was the first favoured port of call, then London, where the most sought-after hotels were those nearest the shopping Mecca of Oxford Street, allowing the quickest possible access to London's chain stores. When London became dearer Glasgow took over, and then the non-touristy Newcastle, liked by those of more modest means as a day trip allowed a shopping expedition without the added expense of a night in a hotel. As soon as the dollar showed signs of weakening, Icelanders headed for the Malls of America, near Minneapolis, the largest retail outlet in the United States. The place may lack the charm of old Europe, but the luggage allowance of 25 kilograms enhanced its attractions.

Motor Culture

Some years ago Iceland overtook the United States in the league table of inhabitants per motor vehicle (or soon, no doubt, vehicles per inhabitant). In 2008 there were 655 vehicles per 1,000 inhabitants, perhaps a world record. Driving lessons can begin at the age of sixteen and the test taken at seventeen, while the right to vote is at eighteen and the right to buy alcohol at the state monopoly shops at twenty. The motor car is indispensable for all but a tiny minority of middle-class intellectuals in the centre of Reykjavik, while the capital (100,000 inhabitants and a total of 200,000 including the surrounding suburbs and satellite towns) is much more spread out than Paris. People use their cars to go to work, to go shopping or to take their children to music classes. The Icelandic mother transforms herself after work into a taxi driver for her offspring while her husband works overtime to pay for the second or third car. The car is both a means of transport and a way of life; it shelters its owner from the winter wind, the slightest sunshine through the windscreen gives the welcome impression of warmth and it gives protection from the ash clouds that since April 2010 have intermittently plagued the country. But the car is also an investment. It is sold so that its owner can go and live abroad or undertake a course of study, in which case one may buy a smaller one. Volvo's advertising slogan for years read "Volvo, a property on four wheels", and this neatly sums up local attitudes towards car ownership.

The average Icelander expects to park his or her car wherever they are going, and town planners have bowed to this expectation (which is in part understandable given the climate). Secondary schools have extensive car parks for the large numbers of students who own cars that they have bought after working during the summer. A hierarchy of vehicles exists, with at the top the jeep, preferably black with darkened windows, which costs the equivalent of several years' pay for an ordinary worker. Then come the more ordinary 4x4 models. Owners have been heard to say, "Buying a jeep at least I know I won't die in a car crash," even though Iceland's road accident statistics are among the best in the world. The number of vehicles has fallen since 2008 although there are always traffic jams on the capital's main intersections during the rush hour.

Money Money Money

Young Icelanders traditionally worked during the summer from the age of fifteen. The days of sending children to the countryside are gone, however, and the crisis has ended the system whereby paid work experience was organized in tandem with studies. As a result the link between education and work has become blurred in recent years, while traditional summer jobs are scarcer or more restricted. Nowadays neither businesses nor shops close over the summer, and it is mainly young people who replace older workers when they take their holiday. Construction, once limited to the summer months, is now an all-year-round activity because of advances in technology and better quality cement, while the fishing sector employs full-time Polish or Asian workers, leaving few seasonal jobs. The young are consequently left with no options other than the service sector, working in shops or restaurants. Yet unlike elsewhere, they rarely depend on hand-outs from their parents and often pay for their own studies or overseas travel. In many cases financial acumen and self-reliance come earlier than intellectual or emotional maturity, and it is not unusual to own a car at the age of seventeen and even—in the fishing communities—for twenty-year-olds to be paying for a new house to be built.

The value system dictates that what is new is beautiful and not what is old or unusual. New models and designs are desirable in terms of furnishing, kitchen décor and cars, while up-to-date fashions are also essential, but especially when bought abroad and preferably in London. There can never be too much redecorating—at Christmas, Easter (the great spring clean), for a child's communion or for a birthday. The cult of the new means that it is difficult to eat in the same Reykjavik restaurant as four years ago, and with the exception of a few established favourites, establishments change hands and appearance with bewildering regularity. A newly-opened restaurant will announce in the media how much its refurbishment cost but will not mention its menu, the expensive makeover being read as the surest sign of its quality.

The tendency in this small society is to do the same thing as others and to do it immediately. Fashions and fads are adopted quickly and disappear just as quickly, especially those adopted from abroad. Icelanders are mockingly self-aware of this trait, famously exemplified in the case of a vibrating machine designed to relieve aching feet which, after a few weeks, was owned by almost every family in Iceland. If in every country in the world young people dress in the same way, this phenomenon affects all generations in Iceland. Not being like everybody else is a matter of social guilt and inspires the expression *Það er til skammar* ("it's a disgrace"), which can be applied to the fact that the car is dirty, the sitting room has not been repainted for four years or the bathtub is scratched. Not to be like everybody else is not a question of law like in an archaic society but implies in its differentiation from others a loss of self-respect.

A visit to the home of rich friends reveals that everything is *lúxus*, as they say in Icelandic, and it must be added *eins og í útlöndum* ("like abroad") and *á heimsmælikvarða* (world class). The obsession with meeting foreign standards betrays a status anxiety that Icelanders like to make fun of themselves, and it suggests why a whole nation allowed itself to be lulled into bankruptcy during the mad years of credit that preceded the crash. Then, at last, Icelanders had "caught up" or, even better, were the best, the most cunning, the most dynamic, the most intelligent, the least corrupt (*sic*) and the happiest people in the world. This illusion was a form of revenge: against the old poverty and colonial domination, against their modest rural origins, against the cold and the endless volcanic eruptions, against everything that had weighed down the people over the centuries.

The boom year created a hitherto unknown type of *nouveau riche*, tasteless but big spending and therefore important for the economy. Preferring quantity to quality, *lúxus* to old-fashioned cachet, the new rich live in suburban areas of Reykjavik where all the roads are dead-ends to preserve their privacy. They have two garages for three cars, a Jacuzzi, a snowmobile, a huge summer house in the country and several horses. They go salmon-fishing and reindeer-hunting. They have a television set in each room and a bathroom of marble or granite but eat very modestly. There is no sign of luxury in their diet until the moment when, in a spotlessly clean house, they organize a party.

Iceland's unusually rich cultural life depends on the hyper-consumerism of its inhabitants. There would not be such a profusion of singers and bands if there were not so many CDs sold, nor so many artists if the walls of the *nouveaux riches* were not covered with paintings. There would be far fewer authors if it was not traditional to give books as Christmas presents. After the financial collapse a number of artists and writers called for a fairer, more honest society, giving more importance to ethical values, to art and to culture. Yet in Reykjavik it seems—although statistics have yet to confirm it—that the crisis has led to a drop in cultural consumption, with the exception of theatre-going.

Icelanders work a good deal and spend even more than they earn. The attitude has always been to spend the fruits of one's labour, to work more in order to spend more, and this attitude was reinforced by a situation of full employment with no fear of a jobless tomorrow. Working and spending have never been seen as opposites, but are rather the two sides of the same coin that represents an outlook on life and a kind of ideal: to be active, dynamic (*duglegur*) and energetic. The national motto might be "I spend therefore I am".

The visitor who has read about Reykjavik's famed nightlife might be surprised when wondering into the city centre between nine in the evening and midnight on a Friday night to see very little going on. He or she might even check to see if they have the right night. But at that time of night the aficionados of Reykjavik's nightlife are still at home, perhaps drinking (as alcohol is much cheaper than in bars). They arrive in town a little before one in the morning and drink until six o'clock alternating alcohol and coffee to keep themselves awake. They return home the worse for wear, sleep until midday two days running and then go back to work ten hours a day. Since the crisis behaviour has changed—but not much. Alcohol sales are down marginally as many can no longer afford such a highly taxed commodity, yet some are surprised that they have not risen as a corollary of the depression that goes with unemployment and mounting debts.

Recovery?

Opinions were divided in 2013 on Iceland's economic prospects. While Europe was sinking further into recession, Iceland was showing clear signs of recovery and growth (an estimated 4.5 per cent in 2012). The greatest success was in reducing unemployment to 5.5 per cent, and if the standard of living was still lower than that in pre-crash 2008, wage rises in 2011 and 2012 were above inflation.

The problems, years after the crash, were still domestic indebtedness and financial uncertainty. The currency controls introduced in 2008 were still in force, and all economists, irrespective of political sympathy, agreed that nothing should be done to change this situation since if restrictions were lifted it was feared that everyone, from individuals to small and larger companies, would speculate against the *króna*.

Iceland has done well from global warming, which inexorably pushes fish stocks further north, including mackerel, which a few years ago was unknown and is now flourishing in Icelandic waters. But the real possibilities lie elsewhere. This is a very young country (if not for long, with declining fertility rates) and a highly optimistic society. Instead of despairing over the harshness of fate, Icelanders—as they like to say—"roll up their sleeves" and work harder. Tourism has not merely grown, but has exploded (a rise of more than 19 per cent in 2012). There are now so many tourists—566,000 in 2011—that their spending outweighs that of Icelandic tourists (domestically and abroad). In Reykjavik they can now choose between dozens of top-quality hotels, a plethora of new bars and restaurants and a nightlife that has become internationally famous.

And Icelanders are also looking further away, towards Greenland to the west, where they hope that they can take part in the mineral extraction boom caused by receding ice. They are looking eastwards, where they want one day to have a role in the new shipping route to the north of Siberia. They are looking north, too, towards the so-called Dragon Zone where, in collaboration with Norway's Petrol company, they hope to find oil in an area well to the north of the polar circle, at depths of more than 1,500 metres and where there is no firm proof of significant reserves—but none of this dampens Icelandic enthusiasm. And finally they are looking south, with a plan to export electricity generated in Iceland to the Faroe Islands and—why not?—to Scotland.

Graffiti on Laugavegur (Christian Bickel/Wikimedia Commons)

11 | The Dark Side
Crime, Calamity and Adversity

One of the clichés repeated by guides and willingly accepted by tourists is that crime is very rare in this huge, sparsely populated land. The tourists are often told the same story: in the Litla-Hraun prison, founded in 1929 and then the only jail in the country, there were some forty prisoners. As there were no guards the prison gate was locked at night, and so those prisoners who headed off during the day to visit the barber or for some other errand had to be careful to return by dusk or face the prospect of sleeping outside. In 1908 the aristocratic British traveller Mrs. Disney Leith reported that "Iceland is a very quiet, law-abiding country, and though there is a prison in Reykjavik, there are hardly ever any prisoners. There used to be only two policemen in Reykjavik. They walked about the town in dark uniforms, looking rather like tin soldiers. Now there are a few more, as the town has increased so much; but there is very little crime."

In contrast, a widespread belief deeply held in Icelandic society is that organized crime is more widespread and powerful than the media will admit. It is certainly true that through respect for privacy, in a society where everyone knows everything about everyone else, the private details of individuals' lives were traditionally not generally on public display. Yet since 2008 this has changed as the economic collapse has shattered most taboos. Some remain, however, not least the way in which death notices and obituaries rarely allude to the cause of death and never mention suicide—which, of course, encourages rumours. When Icelanders were enjoying to excess the delights of the credit card, one such rumour spread through Reykjavik and beyond—that a man had shot himself in the head after gluing a credit card to his forehead. It was pure fiction, of course, and the same apocryphal story was to circulate again after the crash. In fact, the economic crisis has had no impact whatsoever on Icelandic suicide rates.

Crime statistics should be treated with care. As regards to murders, they can increase or decrease from one year to the next by one hundred per cent. In simple terms, however, if there are approximately two murders per hundred thousand inhabitants across Europe, there is only 0.5 in Iceland while some statistics suggest that murder is literally non-existent. The San Diego State University Crime and Society website reports: "According to the INTERPOL data, for murder, the rate in 1998 was 0.00 per 100,000 population for Iceland, 1.10 for Japan, and 6.3 for USA." In 2008, 24 people were serving prison sentences for murder (sixteen years maximum but in reality never more than eight), and a decade before there were only ten. Sentences for possession or dealing in drugs, however, have become more lenient as stricter sentencing had caused an explosion in the prison population of whom many were of Polish or Baltic origins.

There is little cash in circulation in Iceland, as people use a credit card to buy a loaf of bread or a carton of milk, and soon there will only be illegal black-economy work that is paid for in cash. Robberies are rare under these circumstances, and the rarity of money has encouraged a certain form of delinquency where cash is needed immediately. Small stalls where children spend their pocket money on sweets have become targets now that banks conduct most of their operations without banknotes. Pick-pocketing and thefts of valuables from cars, especially in tourist sites, have increased in recent years.

Yet Reykjavik remains a quiet city where people feel safe. A girl can be out alone in the city centre at three in the morning without her parents dying of fear, and if some locals drink a great deal at the weekend and there is a lot of shouting until the early hours of the morning, acts of violence are relatively rare. Twice a year the authorities remind parents of rules and regulations concerning their children. Before the age of thirteen they are allowed to play outside the house until 10 p.m. or 8 p.m. during the winter (adolescents are permitted to stay out longer). The legislation remains very strict in relation to the state-run alcohol outlets but is not always observed to the letter of the law in bars and clubs. The sense of safety in the city centre is perhaps more important than safety itself as Reykjavik is perhaps no more risk-free than other towns or cities of the same size. Even so, the worst excesses committed here have something childlike about them, and there remains a sort of innocence in the depravity. It is only really in Icelandic crime fiction that real evil and vice are to be found.

Drink and Drugs

Drug use is quite significant in Iceland despite supply difficulties. Locals love the excitement of sleepless nights and artificial highs, and when they drink many mix alcohol with caffeine, in the shape of coffee with cognac for the more sophisticated or whisky and coke for more popular tastes. Even the most favoured forms of chocolate are filled with liquorice, a stimulant. Marijuana is smoked widely but most drug users prefer stimulants to sedatives, and heroin is almost unknown not only because of its soporific qualities but because of the small market. Yet before 2008 even the limited market saw a mini-boom as the "New Vikings" found in cocaine the sensation of their invincibility and then consolation in their downfall. Steroids are to be found in the capital's gyms but amphetamines are the narcotic of choice for many, another drug that pushes the limits of physical endurance. This same search for stimulation even used to find expression in the use of tobacco. At sea, when the fish were being unloaded from the nets, smoking a cigarette or taking snuff was impossible, so fishermen used to place snuff between their toes in the belief that the nicotine would enter their bloodstream through the thin layer of skin. Chewing tobacco from Sweden is now the popular alternative to cigarettes.

Drugs come into the country through airline and boat passengers, but some supply is produced locally. Icelanders are adept at greenhouse cultivation, with cheap electricity replacing sunshine, while illegal cultivation is quite easy in a country that is so under-populated. In recent times the police have discovered a number of illicit and half-hidden greenhouses cultivating marijuana. The growers had one incriminating weakness—an above average electricity bill that gave the game away.

Murder in the Sagas

Iceland has not always been a Scandinavian success story of low crime and responsible citizenship. Its early history was written in blood, and we know despite the absence of precise historical sources that its first settlers—such as Ingólfur Arnarson—were outlaws forced to flee Norway after shedding more blood.

Njáls saga was written at the end of the thirteenth century, but the events it recounts are from three centuries earlier. Its author is unknown. The saga unfolds at Fjótshlíð, between the Eyjafjallajökull ice cap and the Hekla volcano, where today information boards, ·often in the open countryside, explain to visitors how to follow the action. Those who have read the text can learn more in the museum devoted to *Njáls saga* in the village of Hvolsvöllur. In the scene below (the translation is by Magnússon and Pálsson), where Njáll is burnt alive in his house, marks the end of fifty years of family feud when Flosi and his men decide to exterminate Njáll and his sons, including Helgi.

Now all of the house began to blaze. Njáll went to the door and said, "Is Flosi near enough to hear my words?"

Flosi said that he could hear him.

Njáll said, "Would you consider making an agreement with my sons, or letting anyone leave the house?"

"I will make no terms with your sons," replied Flosi. "We shall settle matters now, once and for all, and we are not leaving until every one of them is dead. But I shall allow the women and children and servants to come out."

In pagan Iceland women were never executed but whipped, and this tradition continued during the Catholic period until Lutheran reform established a healthy equality between the sexes with both liable for the death penalty—men, however, were beheaded while women were drowned. The saga continues:

Njáll went back inside the house and said to his household: "All those with permission to go out must do so now. Leave the house now, Þórhalla Ásgrímsdóttir, and take with you all those who are allowed to go."

Þórhalla said, "This is not the parting from Helgi I had ever expected, but I urge my father and my brothers to avenge the killings that are committed here."

"You will do well," said Njáll, "for you are a good woman."

She went out, taking many people with her.

Astrid of Djúpriverbank said to Helgi, "Come out with me, I'll drape you in a woman's cloak and put a head-scarf over you."

Helgi protested at first, but finally yielded to their entreaties. Astrid wrapped a scarf round his head, and Þórhildur laid the cloak over his shoulders. Then he walked out between them, along with his sisters Þorgerður and Helga and several other people.

When Helgi came outside, Flosi said, "That's a very tall and broad-shouldered woman—seize her." When Helgi heard this, he threw off the cloak; he was carrying a sword under his arm, and now he struck out at one of the men, slicing off the bottom of the shield and severing his leg. Then Flosi came up and struck at Helgi's neck, cutting off his leg with one blow.

Flosi went up to the door and called Njáll and Bergþóra over to speak to him; when they came, he said, "I want to offer you to come out, for you do not deserve to burn."

"I have no wish to go outside," said Njáll, "for I am an old man now and ill-equipped to avenge my sons; and I do not want to live in shame."

Flosi said to Bergþóra, "You come out, Bergþóra, for under no circumstances do I want you to burn."

Bergþóra replied, "I was given to Njáll in marriage when young, and I have promised him that we would share the same fate."

Then they both went back inside.

"What shall we do now?" asked Bergþóra.

"Let us go to our bed," said Njáll, "and lie down."

Then Bergþóra said to little Þórður, Kári's son, "You are to be taken out. You are not to burn."

The boy replied, "But that's not what you promised, grand-mother. You said that we would never be parted; and so it shall be, for I would much prefer to die beside you both."

She carried the boy to the bed. Njáll said to his steward, "Take note where we lay ourselves down, and how we dispose ourselves, for I shall not move from here however much the smoke of flames distress me. Then you can know where to look for our remains."

The steward said he would.

An ox had recently been slaughtered, and the hide was lying nearby. Njáll told the steward to spread the hide over them, and he promised to do so.

Njáll and Bergþóra lay down on the bed and put the boy between them. Then they crossed themselves and the boy, and com-mended their souls to God. These were the last words they were heard to speak.

Njáls saga is one of the last of the genre, written when Icelanders had already adopted Christianity, as is clear in Njáll's final words.

A Sixteenth-Century Serial Killer

A play by Björn Hlynur Haraldsson that premiered in Reykjavik in 2012 retraced the extraordinary life of the "serial killer" Axlar Björn, whose sixteenth-century exploits were recorded by the priest Sveinn Níelsson (1801-81) and inspired several folk tales by Jón Árnason (1819-88). Named Axlar after the genitive form of Öxl, the farm where he grew up near Búðir in the Snæfellsnes peninsula, Björn (his first name) was reputed to have inherited his diabolical nature from his mother, who when pregnant yearned for human blood. After a series of weird omens he married and became a farmer. As was the contemporary custom, farmers were expected to feed and give shelter to passing travellers, but those who stayed with Björn, it seems, had little chance of leaving his house alive. It is thought that he murdered eighteen people before his attempt to kill a brother and sister led to his downfall. Another version has it that a wandering woman with three children stopped at the farmhouse and that Björn killed the children before the woman reported him to the local sheriff.

Björn's wife Þórdís was allegedly his accomplice, and the annals report that when he was not strong enough to murder on his own she would strangle the victims with twine and bludgeoned them with a club. The motive was apparently theft. All the victims were thrown into the pond by the farm.

Axlar Björn was condemned to death in 1596, his bones broken with a sledgehammer before he was beheaded and his limbs hung from poles. Þórdís was not tried at the same time as she was pregnant but was nevertheless beaten. Their son Sveinn seemingly followed in the family tradition as he was hanged in 1648 for raping a farmer's wife who fought back and brought him to justice, and the family saga was brought to end when Sveinn's son was also hanged.

Axlar Björn was a unique case and quite probably mentally ill, but like all historical "monsters" the nature of his crimes, his methods and his eventual punishment reveal much about the period in question.

Poverty, Famine and Disasters

Over the next two centuries Iceland slid further into poverty and despair. Temperatures fell during what is known as the "little ice age" (c.1550-c.1850) and it became impossible to cultivate cereals. Meanwhile, the Danish authorities imposed a monopoly on all imports and exports and it was even forbidden for farmers and other producers to trade among themselves. Then eruption in 1783 of the Laki volcanic system in the Vatnajökull glacier produced devastating flows of lava and vast poisonous clouds that left the country in darkness. An earthquake followed in 1784, and the winters of 1783 and 1784 were lethal due to the sulphur dioxide that killed an estimated fifty per cent of the country's livestock. Those who survived the ash clouds often died of starvation (an estimated quarter of the Icelandic population perished, while crop failures across Europe may have led to some six million deaths). Such was the gravity of the situation that the Danes, according to one disputed source, even considered evacuating the entire population to Denmark. It was a crushing blow for Icelanders and many opposed the plan. Demographic statistics reveal the full extent of the catastrophe: the population, estimated at 70,000 in the twelfth century, was lower than 40,000 at the end of the eighteenth.

The Laki eruption was not to be the last, and even today Icelanders live in fear of another natural disaster. That of the unpronounceable Eyjafjallajökull in 2010 and 2011 was felt in Reykjavik, over 120 kilometres away, where ash covered streets and gardens. Yet this eruption, which delayed and disturbed international flights with its drifting ash plume, also had unexpected consequences. Tourism figures in 2009 had been mediocre and professionals feared that fears of a fresh eruption would deter visitors. In fact, the opposite was true as tourist arrivals increased in 2010, perhaps spurred by the free international advertising produced by Eyjafjallajökull.

Blood Crimes

The Icelandic crime *par excellence* is that of incest. It is to be found in the theatre, in the cinema and in literature, and is often the subject of sensationalist newspaper stories, revealed by the victims after the death of the abuser. Sometimes the abuse occurs between a step-father or an adoptive father and a child—not real incest but still explored morbidly by the media.

One of the most famous novels of the inter-war period, Gunnar Gunnarsson's (1889-1975) *Svartfugl* (*The Black Bird*) tells of a criminal affair that is not incest but is no less a drama of illicit promiscuity. The story takes place in the nineteenth century and revolves around two farming couples who share the same isolated house in the remote western fjords. An adulterous relationship occurs, and the story ends with the death of the errant woman's husband, the confession of the murderer and his execution.

It is in the many Icelandic detective novels, however, that most crimes are committed. This genre, part of the fashionable "Nordic Noir", often conforms to the generalized outside cliché of Iceland as a bleak, isolated outpost of depressives, battling to survive a semi-permanent winter (it goes without saying that this is not the Icelanders' view of themselves). In the novels of writers such as Arnaldur Indriðason (featuring the detective Erlendur), Yrsa Sigurðardóttir and Viktor Arnar Ingólfsson the bizarre and the gory are commonplace. According to the critic Barbara Fister, the plot of *Voices* (Reykjavik Murder Mysteries 3)

> involves the detectives in uncovering the life history of the victim, a doorman living in a shabby room in the basement of a huge hotel. Once a year he plays Santa Claus for the tourists; this time, though, he's found stabbed to death, his pants around his ankles, a condom drooping from his penis. As the police delve into his past, Erlendur muses on the contrast between the tourist version of Iceland and the reality.

Some, meanwhile, might argue that Iceland's real criminals are not to be found in the country's prisons, but are at large, protected by an army of lawyers. The money they have acquired, legally or not, is safely deposited in the British Virgin Islands, Luxemburg or Switzerland, and although they choose to live in Geneva or London they return to Iceland from time to time, hidden behind the darkened windows of 4x4s and waiting to asset strip another bankrupt firm.

2008: Icelanders Discover Political Violence

The fight for independence had been very peaceful, with nobody killed and no one injured. The only instance of political violence in the country's modern history took place in 1949 in front of the parliament when demonstrators protested against NATO membership. Then came the crisis of 2008. The Canadian professor Daniel Chartier describes in *The End of Iceland's Innocence* how an eruption of violence following the collapse of the economy surprised locals and journalists alike:

> The protests and violence surprised foreign commentators. "These are highly unusual events in Iceland, normally a very reserved society," reported the BBC. Even from the inside they appeared exceptional, prompting the editor in chief of *Iceland Review* to write: "fighting in the streets of Reykjavik, it was not the Iceland I know. But then again, what has happened here in the past months is not the Iceland I know either." In fact, according to the *Economist*, "such protests are almost unheard of: the only previous mass demonstrations to shake the country, against NATO membership, took place in 1949."
>
> The events caused a shift in the media coverage. Suddenly newspapers began quoting some Icelanders' statements about revolutions in other parts of the world. One financially ruined pensioner spoke to the *Financial Times* of revolution in a wry tone:
>
> "The Icelandic people are too lazy," he says. "Why don't we go to the airport and block it until we get answers? For the first time in my life I have sympathy with the Bolsheviks; with the French revolutionaries who put up the guillotine."
>
> Journalists from London and Paris, used to rowdy riots, looked upon the small Icelandic demonstrations with amusement and condescension, comparing them with "squabbles". *Le Monde* reported a good-natured crowd of protesters making noise with kitchen pots and musical instruments as police intervened, making a bad impression: "The police, numerous but inexperienced, grasped their transparent shields, soon dripping with broken eggs and dairy products." The BBC commented ironically on the "reinforcements" posted in front of the Parliament: "It is a sign of the times that security has been increased at Reykjavik's small Parliament building, from one policeman to three." *The Australian*, however, took this increased security seriously and interpreted it as a loss of innocence for Iceland. But it too was impressed by the newly deployed security at the Reykjavik exchange: "Half joking, half serious, a new security guard blocked the journalist's path. It was one of his first days in the job. Before trading was shut down last week the exchange was not guarded."

A new left-wing government, led by Prime Minister Jóhanna Sigurðardóttir, was constituted in spring 2009. The demonstrations faded away. A peaceful meeting was nevertheless held every Saturday in front of the *Althing* for a few months after the events. Two demonstrators were eventually charged despite the prime minister herself protesting that the two young men were the only individuals to be convicted in a process that had involved all parts of society during many months. Yet justice needed to make an example. The day, 8 December 2008, was chosen at random, nine people were arrested out of fifty and two condemned at the end. The lawsuit was first postponed because the *Althing*'s employee who charged the two young men was the sister-in-law of the public prosecutor. It was a classic case of promiscuity.

Selfoss waterfall, northern Iceland (Max Topchii/Shutterstock)

12 | **Escape**
Suburbs and Surroundings

Only forty years ago, lava fields separated Reykjavik properly from its surrounding settlements, but now the spread of urbanization has brought them together. All the municipalities share a single bus network, which enables passengers to travel more or less anywhere for the price of a single fare. How could it be otherwise in such a small and thinly populated agglomeration? Buses generally arrive on time, the drivers usually speak English and the names of the stops are shown on an electronic panel. As free transfers, valid for up to 75 minutes, are available, it makes sense to tour the suburbs of Reykjavik by bus.

Seltjarnarnes

Reykjavik stands on a promontory whose tip it cedes to an independent township, Seltjarnarnes (literally "seal lake cape"), which stretches towards the sea and comes to an end with a golf course and an island and lighthouse, accessible at low tide, called Grótta. It offers a pleasant walk in good weather, and Seltjarnarnes also boasts a swimming pool of filtered sea water and a small pool of warm water close to the sea. There is little in the way of temptation here and no nightlife, with only a shopping centre and a single bar to entertain the inhabitants. Its independence has long allowed the town to take advantage of different local laws from those in force in Reykjavik. Indeed, this windswept and barren community considers itself separate from and perhaps superior to the capital. Dogs were allowed there when they were banned from the capital from 1924 to the end of the 1980s (a move taken to combat Echinococcosis), and when shops were shut in Reykjavik on Sundays the grocery at Seltjarnarnes, situated a few metres from the dividing line between the two towns, was always open.

Seltjarnarnes is a prosperous place, and living there is a sign of social status, even if residents are regularly buffeted by the sea winds, which blow in from every conceivable direction. Trees grow with considerable difficulty, but many who live there feel that the climate is a price worth paying for the sense of exclusivity and neighbourliness, for everyone knows more or less everyone else in Seltjarnarnes. Here—perhaps due to the lack of trees—every movement is scrutinized and private life is hard to keep private, so any aspiring politician would be well advised to live elsewhere.

To the South

For many years **Kópavogur** was a planning disaster, cut in half by the motorway that joins the airport to the capital and losing its heart in the process. To the west is the prettier part, forming a cape surrounded by calm waters. This end of Kópavogur ("sea pup bay") is a promontory like Seltjarnarnes and is sheltered to the west by Álftanes the Bessastaðir peninsula and to the north by Reykjavik. In the 1960s Kópavogur was still a big village, and people would go to live there to feel that they were in the countryside and because land prices were cheap. It was said at the time that Kópavogur voted more to the left than Reykjavik, as those who had settled there were Iceland's poorest community.

For many years the modern church (with windows by Leifur Breiðfjörð) was Kópavogur's only attraction, but the situation has now changed. A road tunnel, which the civil engineers had always wanted, was finally built to reunite the west and the east of the town, and development and growth have followed. Only Reykjavik enjoys the status of city (*borg*) but Kópavogur, with its population of some 35,000, has for some time aspired to match it. If most locals, conversely, look to the nearby capital for fun and excitement, two establishments in Kópavogur try to attract custom from outside the town. A bar carries the name Catalina in tribute to the only female brothel keeper prosecuted in Iceland, while Goldfinger, banished to a shabby industrial estate, is known for its erotic dancers and its clientele of surreptitious men. Once situated in Reykjavik, this club was persecuted by the capital's upholders of moral standards and was forced to move to Kópavogur. The "poor girls", whose exploitation was condemned by the club's opponents, gained little from the move, as it is certainly safer to leave work in a striptease bar at night in the centre of Reykjavik than in a suburban industrial estate.

With its burgeoning population, Kópavogur has equipped itself with several prestigious cultural institutions: an excellent concert hall (Salurinn) and an interesting art gallery next door. At the peak of its megalomaniacal phase (in 2008, before the crash), the town even planned to build an opera house. Fortunately the plans remained on the drawing board, as Reykjavik's pharaonic Harpa concert hall amply caters to the needs of opera enthusiasts, who barely fill the auditorium a few times a year. Yet the town's greatest draw is its gigantic Smáralind shopping centre, home to over seventy shops and restaurants. This temple to mass consumption is hard to reach in a confusing maze of motorway exits and slip-roads, but seen from an airplane it has the unmistakable appearance of a vast horizontal phallus. A nearby indoor full-size football pitch is further witness to previous civic delusions of grandeur. The former mayor, involved in the construction industry, was voted out in the last municipal elections by an improvised centre-left coalition, one member of which was the unusually named Second Best Party (Næstbesti flokkurinn), headed by an actor. The protest group was clearly inspired by the Best Party (Besti flokkurinn), which enjoyed electoral success in Reykjavik in 2010.

Taking the infamous motorway that now runs underground through central Kópavogur, the first municipality to be reached is **Garðabær**. This is an American-style suburb *par excellence*, with dead-end residential roads with a turning space at the end—for those drivers who have lost their way. Each house has a double garage, but its rear is perhaps more attractive, where a vast living room is usually extended by a large terrace protected by wooden wind-breaks. This is the realm of the barbecue for outdoor meals in summer. The decor may be American but the fittings are strictly determined by the Icelandic climate, where the average temperature in July, when night and day are more or less indistinguishable, is a mere 12°C and it often rains. Hence a marquee provides shelter and a gas heater combats the evening chill.

The suburban family may well have a second house in the countryside within a 100-kilometre radius of Reykjavik. Here there will be another sheltered terrace, another barbecue and neighbours no further away than those in their Garðabær street. Why such proximity in a country where population density stands at three inhabitants per square kilometre? The reason lies in the fact that the necessities of modern life—electricity, hot water, television—are only affordable if cost of power lines, pipes and cables is shared between a big group of residents.

Leaving Garðabær, whose secrets remain undiscovered (only occasionally residents are to be seen walking, or rather jogging, on its streets), the main road to the right leads towards **Bessastaðir**, site of the official residence of Iceland's president. There is no wall or fence around the property, and visitors are free to approach the modest main building with its adjoining church. This is where all incoming governments pose for a photograph with the president, and the arrival of these guests often has a comic touch as the wind always blows particularly fiercely here and many a woman who has spent the whole afternoon at the hairdresser has been discomfited by sudden violent blasts. Some presidents have chosen to live here, and others have merely used the building for receptions.

In the past the Norwegian, then Danish governors ruled from here, but were often conspicuous by their absence, these emblematic figures of colonial power only residing during the short summer season. In fact, this colonial power, which was remembered as authoritarian and grasping by its Icelandic subjects, was remarkably absent. Psychoanalysis has taught us that the feeling of abandonment is more painful than that of oppression, and what Icelanders have never forgiven their Danish masters was their indifference.

Further south from Garðabær lies the pretty fishing port of **Hafnarfjörður**, still a busy maritime centre although now abandoned by the fish processing factories. On the slope overlooking the port old wooden houses are built on the lava fields, which are still visible in places. These houses are less perfect; more modestly restored than their Reykjavik counterparts, and thus create a sense of tradition and authenticity.

Jokes about Hafnarfjörður (*Hafnarfjarðarbrandarar*) abound in Iceland, similar to those told at the expense of Irish, Belgians and so on and revolving around the inhabitants' alleged naivety. Many are based on puns only comprehensible to Icelanders. Needless to say, these jokes rarely raise a smile in Hafnarfjörður whose people, eternally mocked, have developed a resilient sort of local pride. The thermometer at the petrol station at the entrance to the town, which some believe may be optimistically adjusted, allows them to claim with proof that their town has the best climate in the country. They also like to claim that until recently residents had no need to lock their houses as the township had no crime (though more than twenty years ago they were also saying "until recently").

The town, the country's third biggest, is undeniably a pleasant place, with a stream running through it, which, unlike in Reykjavik, has not been covered over and the feeling that the sea is always close. The Hafnarborg in the town centre is a museum and performance centre, and the visitor can have coffee, watch the fishing boats and explore the main street. Another more debatable attraction is the Viking Village, a complex of hotel, cottages and restaurants that aims to recreate elements of Viking culture. Disbelief has to be suspended as the place is more fantasy than historic reality, but its artificiality does not prevent many from having fun.

All visitors as well as locals are familiar with **Keflavik**, the first or last place to be seen when arriving or departing by airplane, but few visit the town itself with its naval installations and fishing port. Now incorporated into the municipality of Reykjanesbær, Keflavik remains the prisoner of its reputation: the site of the American military base, both a source of employment and opportunity and the object of ambivalent feelings. Now gone (the last NATO personnel left in 2006), the base was a closed world, inspiring mystery, longing and scorn. Jobs were easy to find, but at the risk of being ostracized by friends and family, while young women who were tempted by the idea of escape could find themselves reviled as prostitutes.

Some apartments still remain, turned into student accommodation, but the abandoned hangars have yet to find takers. The presence of the NATO base for 55 years divided opinion in Iceland, a country that never had its own military, and anti-base feeling ran highest during the Vietnam War. Several thousand demonstrators walked the forty kilometres from Keflavik to the capital; with the less fit joining the march along the way. It is hard to imagine the demonstration on today's motorway.

Those in favour of the base, despite their pro-American sympathies, never held the US and NATO troops in high regard. A symbol of an opulent society in the post-war years, the base gradually diminished in importance as Icelanders became wealthier. After the construction (financed by the US) of a civilian airport on the base, the separation between military and population was almost complete.

The Blue Lagoon

Leaving Keflavik on the road back to the capital, the first right turn is the road to Grindavík, an interesting fishing village and the only one on the south coast of the Reykjanes peninsula. Before the village is a turn-off to the Blue Lagoon, one of Iceland's biggest attractions. Some enthuse about the site, while others consider it a tourist trap. In either case the origins of this spa, strangely, are entirely accidental. Iceland's geothermal potential, as we have seen, is almost infinite, while at the same time the country requires large amounts of salt for the processing of cod. The Svartsengi Power Station was constructed in the 1970s with the aim of exploiting both resources: the station generated electricity from hot saltwater from deep below the lava field, while salt was produced by evaporating the water with the heat generated. The by-product of silica mud was dumped onto the surrounding lava along with mineral-rich hot water.

Salt production turned out to be a failure, and fish processing plants returned to the coarser variety that gives the salt cod its typical appearance. But the surrounding ponds had by now taken on an eerie blue quality, and it was claimed that the waters had a therapeutic effect, notably against the skin condition psoriasis.

What had become a large lagoon was fenced in and a rudimentary swimming pool was opened. The changing rooms were primitive, the cost of entrance modest and the general atmosphere eccentric. Some sought relief not from psoriasis but from hangovers, the fence was easy to climb and two drunken men were drowned within a short space of time.

Something had to be done, and redevelopment moved the bathing pool away from the power station and its noise. A new landscape was created, but the surrounding lava field is still entirely authentic. The Blue Lagoon complex now includes a health centre, a sauna and café, and more than 400,000 tourists visit each year to sit or lie in the milky, aqua blue waters as they simmer and steam at temperatures between 37 and 39°C. Icelanders tend to visit during the winter at reduced rates, while foreign tourists are bussed to the site all year-round, often on their way to the airport at Keflavik. Covering oneself in the pool's white mud is a unique pleasure, as is sitting in hot, if somewhat sulphurous, water, surrounded by a snow-covered wilderness. At dusk the interplay of colours—aquamarine, black and white—is magical.

Heiðmörk

Returning towards Reykjavik, there are plenty of navigable dirt roads leading down to the sea on the northern coast of the peninsula. The variety of marine life never fails to impress, and if there is little hope of swimming in the freezing waters, there is the pleasure of finding mussels, starfish and anemones on wild and deserted shores.

Back in Garðabær, a road to the right takes us in the direction of **Vífilsstaðir**, a large and forbidding white structure built in 1910 for tuberculosis patients and then used as a centre for the detoxification of alcoholics. Here one ostracized group has been replaced by another, yet detox, under the auspices of Alcoholics Anonymous, is a flourishing activity in Iceland (involving up to five per cent of the population)—a strange development given that Icelanders consume the least alcohol *per capita* in Europe after the Turkish. Some wonder whether these detox cures are in fact related to drunkenness or are rather more rites of purification, catharsis, a mix of fitness training and monastic retreat. Patients may go to get over a divorce or to save on the expense of a course of psychoanalysis, and in this sense alcohol is seen less as a disorder in itself than as the symptom of a greater disorder. If in Iceland drink is commonly viewed as the cause of all personality defects, it is more often than not merely the consequence.

Icelanders are generally not drinkers (half have never drunk or only drink twice a year) but collectively they are happy with their image as heavy drinkers, this being the favourite weakness among the characteristics that they attach to themselves. And, indeed, alcohol plays an important social role, the same as with the Faroese. In the small social microcosm it provides a sort of freedom in which what one says will not be held against one. It is less boredom or inactivity than a two-tier system, where work and conformity—restrictive and open to scrutiny—is counterbalanced by the liberating inebriation of Saturday night, when emotions are released and all sorts of misbehaviour are tolerated. At that moment the drinker is no longer aware of being watched, even if he is still with others.

Past Vífilsstaðir is the large lake known as **Vífilsstaðavatn**, which offers pleasant walks around the water's edge or on the surrounding hills, especially when the lupins are in flower. Further along the road are the Maríuhellar lava caves and then the **Heiðmörk** municipal conservation area, an eleven square-kilometre network of tracks that crisscross a densely wooded area. Nowadays foresters plant the tree species that grow best, notably Alaskan black cottonwood and pine, alder and silver birch, but before many experiments were undertaken, and Heiðmörk was at the centre of reforestation research. Species that appear in the main mountain areas across Europe have been planted, and the combination of salt, wind, frequent frosts and volcanic soil has meant that some have prospered better than others.

A little further on, the road turns to the left (where a cairn on the right is a useful landmark) and a small car park allows visitors to head off cross-country towards **Búrfellsgjá**, famous for its volcanic crater and lava tunnel. The path passes by landslides, fissures and narrow gorges or cave entrances that are not dangerous but demand concentration. It slowly follows the course of a tunnel that becomes increasingly narrow, a former cave whose roof collapsed in the distant past and which was formed when a lava flow followed the course of a stream. At the end of the enclosed track, watched over by rocky crags, comes the reward: it emerges at the edge of a volcanic crater, a remnant of an eruption that is thought to have occurred some eight thousand years ago. Fragments of ancient cinder lie scattered around the site, while from the top of the crater, 180 metres above sea level, one can make out the buildings of Reykjavik, the Reykjanes peninsula, the Esja mountain range and the massifs to the west.

Walkers are likely to find themselves alone in this spectacular spot, where the tunnel offers some protection from the wind. Only fifteen kilometres from the city, it is a place of unspoilt nature and vast skies. Returning to the road, a detour leads past the stone enclosures where sheep were once kept. There are no longer any sheep; the Heiðmörk conservation area is rigorously protected.

Mountain and Lake

For distant views of Reykjavik and its suburbs the road to **Akranes** is another good choice, particularly when the north wind is blowing as Esja offers welcome protection from its biting gusts. Those deterred by more demanding climbs can ascend the more manageable 295 metre **Úlfarsfell**; the path starts above the new eastern suburb of Grafarholt, one of the victims of the 2008 crash, many of whose houses are empty or unfinished. The path is easy and the effort is worthwhile, for the view encompasses the whole of Reykjavik to the west, while the mountains encircling the lake at Þingvellir seem within touching distance.

The more energetic may want to climb Esja itself, where a well demarcated and maintained path starts at sea level and rises to eight hundred metres. Information panels punctuate each stage of the ascent, and it is June, when the lupins bloom en masse, that the walk is most beautiful, though it can be done at any time of year, even in winter for those who like snow. But then the climber should be aware that night falls at 3.30 p.m. A bus route runs to the foot of the Esja range and the beginning of the path.

A car is needed, on the other hand, for an excursion from the north to the south of the Reykjanes peninsula passing by Lake **Kleifarvatn**, the third biggest in Iceland and reaching depths of almost a hundred metres. The landscape here, as the old cliché has it, is lunar—or at least what we imagine the moon to look like. The nearby geothermal area of **Krýsuvík** boasts hot springs and fumaroles that are the equal of the more famous Geyser area (see below). The visitor can take the same road back towards Reykjavik or follow the coast towards **Grindavík** and then to the Blue Lagoon.

The Golden Circle

The so-called Golden Circle, which covers an approximately three-hundred-kilometre loop to the east of Reykjavik, is, after the Blue Lagoon, Iceland's biggest tourist attraction, and there are innumerable ways of making the tour: by rented car, coach or even cycle. Probably the easiest option is to rent a car as the roads present no problems, and it is best to make the excursion between May and October when there is no risk of snow. Many locals prefer to start their tour of the Golden Circle in mid-afternoon on a Sunday in spring or summer, as it is in the evening that the quality of light is at its highest. Of the three main sites that make up the itinerary—**Geysir**, the **Gullfoss** Waterfall and the **Þingvellir** National Park—Geysir is most likely to be crowded as space there is relatively limited, and it is preferable to reach there at the end of the day as the tourist expeditions head back for dinner in Reykjavik. The tour can, of course, be done in either direction.

Leaving Reykjavik on the road south (1) to **Hveragerði**, a left turn (431) takes us to the geothermal power station of **Nesjavellir**, opened in 1990 and whose metallic funnels send steam high above the bleak plain. The recently built road follows the pipes that provide the capital with supplies of hot water. Nesjavellir is a noisy place with its roar of emerging vapour and its network of pipes and boreholes, but several paths have been laid out with information panels. When snow is deep and the painted signs have disappeared there are poles to guide walkers, but the sheep, which have created thousands of smaller paths, make it all too easy for those ramblers who are unfamiliar with the area to take the wrong track into the wilderness.

Roads flank Þingvallavatn or Lake Þingvellir to the north leading to the national park, but bearing south (360 and 36) and then left (35) takes us to the crater lake known as **Kerið**, probably formed some three millennia ago by the sudden and enormous eruption of a cone volcano. This event left a steep-walled crater of red volcanic rock covered in places with moss and containing at its bottom a surprisingly blue lake about ten metres deep. The site is private, but most coaches on the Golden Circle circuit stop there long enough for photographs to be taken. The more courageous visitor can walk around the rim of the crater on a well-signed but vertiginous path. For some reason, the owners, perhaps in a bad mood, forbade the visiting Chinese prime minister from visiting in 2011.

At the junction by **Laugarvatn** (via 37) one can go left to Þingvellir or right (37) towards Gullfoss and Geysir. The choice may depend on the weather as Gullfoss and Geysir are worth seeing even in the rain, while Þingvellir requires brightness and good visibility for visitors to fully appreciate the huge vistas and spectacular landscapes. Laugarvatn, with its imposing university-run sports facilities and school, is a good example of how education was organized in rural areas. School buildings were situated far from towns and students were normally boarders. These school buildings have now, in many cases, been turned into hotels as educational centres have been moved into small towns with school buses replacing the boarding system.

On the road to Gullfoss and Geysir via a short detour (35) is the village of **Reykholt**, a small settlement with many hot springs, greenhouses and a warm swimming pool. From **Úthlíð**, a little further along the road, however, one can survey the countryside from the comfort of a heated pool as the facility is located on a hillside. Trade unions own summer houses on the hill here that they let to their members all year round but especially during the summer season, a period when the leisure centre comes to life.

The **Faxi waterfall** offers a foretaste of what awaits a little further to the west. There is a fine view from the promontory that stands above the falls, the site is likely to be much less crowded than Gullfoss and it is easy to climb down to admire at closer hand the falls, which are wide rather than high and which carry melted snow as well as many streams towards the sea. Faxi may be less impressive than its famous neighbour, but its location, with an ancient ford and sheep fold nearby, is peaceful and suitable for picnics.

Geysir (from the Icelandic word *geysa*, "to gush") is the name given both to an individual hot spring (now dormant) and an area of geothermal activity consisting of other geysers—the English form of the word—as well as mud pots, warm streams and sulphurous steam emissions. Accounts of the Great Geysir itself date back to the thirteenth century, and it was a popular attraction in the nineteenth when it regularly blasted eighty-metre jets of boiling water into the air. Since 1916, however, it has been largely quiet, with only occasional eruptions, and the main attraction is the nearby **Strokkur** (The Churn), which erupts to heights of about thirty metres every ten minutes or so. Each eruption is preceded by an eerie seething of the water within the vent which sinks before shooting upwards. Visitors can stand quite close to the geyser, but it is advisable to gauge the wind direction. Other spouts nearby are less dramatic, and there are myriad pools, some deep blue.

Situated six kilometres from Geysir, **Gullfoss** (Golden Falls) is an iconic landmark and has been wonderfully preserved despite the advent of mass tourism—a fact appreciated by those who have visited the commercially dominated Niagara Falls. It is due to Sigríður Tómasdóttir that the site can be admired in its near-pristine state today; she was the daughter of the landowner and fought first her father and then the government to stop the construction of a hydro-electric dam in the 1920s.

No two visits to Gullfoss are the same as the falls alter in appearance and mood with the changing of the seasons. The volume of water from the **Hvítá** river is greatest in springtime when snow is melting most rapidly, but in deepest winter the falls can appear to be frozen, even though water is still running under the fantasmagoric formations of ice. Gullfoss has none of the symmetry of other Icelandic waterfalls, as if nature had made a design error, and the water does not fall directly down into the riverbed below but at an angle. It plunges in two distinct stages at right angles to each other, and from a distance the water simply seems to disappear as it hurtles into a crevice. The effect of the falls' contortions is to induce vertigo, but it also creates their unique beauty.

On leaving, having visited Geysir's smart tourist shop, it is advisable to adopt the tastes of an average Icelandic family and to stop for an ice cream (even if it is below freezing outside). Even better are SS-brand hotdogs, *með öllu*, in other words "with everything": fried onions, ketchup, mustard and *remúlaði* (mayonnaise with relish). Since the 2008 crisis austerity has changed some habits, and now a thermos of tea or coffee and homemade sandwiches are again popular.

The roads back towards Reykjavik (35, 37, 365 and 36) take us to the **Þingvellir National Park** (see Chapter 3), a place of extraordinary beauty that is rich in both historical interest and geological variety. It has been a protected national park since 1928. An interactive visitor centre at **Hakið** (where, strangely, are to be found Iceland's only pay toilets) provides remarkably detailed and free information on all aspects of the park in several languages. A little way from it is a viewing platform looking over the vast expanse of Þingvallavatn, the largest natural lake in Iceland, from which, to the right, emerges a small, dormant volcano. Icelanders are invariably moved by the site partly because it seems to evoke their glorious past, but also because it exudes a sense of calm, harmony and fullness that they particularly enjoy. Foreign visitors may not encounter the same emotions, but the ideal experience is to see the park in the middle of the day and then to return at dusk when the landscape is bathed in a magical light.

After taking in the view, visitors can walk down to **Almannagjá**, perhaps the most dramatic feature of the UNESCO-recognized national park. An eight kilometre long escarpment, it stands at the eastern boundary of the North American plate and is the largest tectonic fissure—the place where the tectonic plates of Europe and North America are slowly moving apart—in the area. Almannagjá ("public ravine") was the site of the *Althing*, and a flagpole now indicates where it is thought the lawspeaker and the law council gathered with the chieftains. It was here that Iceland's independence was symbolically proclaimed in 1944, nearly 150 years after the remnants of parliament were disbanded in 1800. The acoustics are still remarkable, and it is fascinating to imagine how the 39 *goðar* or leaders lived in their temporary encampments during the two-week *Althing* session. The chieftains probably camped by the crystal-clear **Öxará** river, where a bridge marks a place where a deep pool was used to drown adulterous women and those guilty of infanticide. A list of their names can be seen, not to cast opprobrium but to emphasize the cruelty of a punishment that had nothing to do with Viking law but dates from the era of eighteenth-century puritan extremism.

Several paths lead to a chapel, with its next-door parsonage, and a national graveyard where the poets Einar Benediktsson and Jónas Hallgrímsson are buried. The honour accorded to two poets (and not two politicians) underlines the importance accorded by Iceland to culture and language in its struggle for emancipation.

Nearby is **Flosagjá**, a fissure flooded by underground springs that have created **Peningagjá** ("coin fissure"), a very deep pool where coins thrown in by visitors can be seen lying in the depths. The pool is extremely dangerous as several divers have been killed here. Shortly after the bridge one reaches the spot where the painter Jóhannes Kjarval (see Chapter 6) set up his tent to paint the landscapes and textures of the area.

Ideally, the visitor would also have time to stay and camp in the designated areas within the park. Another option would be to devote a day to exploring the isolated **Kaldidalur** road (550), linking Þingvallavatn and **Borgarfjörður** to the north via the Icelandic Highlands. There is hardly a house on this empty forty-kilometre track, which is in theory accessible by ordinary cars. The expression "the middle of nowhere" fits the road, which winds its way between mountains and glaciers.

Returning to Reykjavik from Þingvellir, the road passes the slopes of Esja before reaching **Gljúfrasteinn**, the home where Nobel Prize laureate Halldór Laxness lived for more than fifty years. It can be visited, and a multimedia presentation explores the writer's life and work. Outside stands his 1968 white Jaguar. From here it is a short drive to the much-developed satellite town of **Mosfellsbær**, situated in a mountainous and geothermally active district, and then back to Reykjavik.

Further Reading and Useful Websites

Aðalskipulag Reykjavikur 1962-83, Master Plan for Reykjavik. Reykjavik: The City of Reykjavik, 1966

Auden, W. H. and MacNeice, Louis, *Letters from Iceland.* London: Faber and Faber, 1985

Auðunsdóttir, Lóa (ed.), *Children's Reykjavik.* Reykjavik: Salka. 2008

Baring-Gould, Sabine, *Iceland: Its Scenes and Sagas.* 1863. Oxford: Signal Books, 2007

Berg, Steinar. *The Last Troll.* Trans. Bernard Scudder. Reykjavik: JPV, 2007

Chartier, Daniel, *The End of Iceland's Innocence: The Image of Iceland in the Foreign Media during the Crisis.* London/Reykjavik: Citizen Press, 2011

Hjort, Mette and Petrie, Duncan (eds.), *The Cinema of Small Nations.* Edinburgh: Edinburgh University Press, 2007

Ellenberger, Íris, *Íslandskvikmyndir 1916-1966.* Reykjavik: Sagnfræðistofnun Háskóla Íslands, 2007

Fergus, Charles, *Summer at Little Lava: A Season at the Edge of the World.* New York: Farrar, Straus & Giroux, 1998

Hákonardóttir, Inga Huld, *Fjarri hlýju hjónasængur : Öðruvísi Íslandssaga.* Reykjavik: Uglan, 1992

Haarberg, Erlend, and Haarberg, Orsolya (photographs), Jökulsdóttir, Unnur (text), *Iceland in all its Splendour.* Reykjavik, Forlagið, 2012

Hall, Richard, *Exploring the World of the Vikings.* London: Thames &Hudson, 2007

Icelandic Documentaries: Short and animated films 1966-1991. Reykjavik: The Icelandic Film Fund, 1991

Icelandic Films. Reykjavik: The Icelandic Film Fund, 1993

Icelandic Films. Reykjavik: The Icelandic Film Fund, 1995

Karlsson, Gunnar, *Iceland's 1100 Years: The History of a Marginal Society.* London: C. Hurst, 2001

Landshagir: Statistical Yearbook of Iceland. Reykjavik: Statistics Iceland, 2009

Leffman, David and Proctor, James, *Iceland: the Rough Guide.* London: Rough Guides, 2001

Lemarquis, Gérard, *Frauskar íslandsvísur: Poésies d'Islande.* Reykjavik: Þýðingaútgáfan, 1981

Lemarquis, Gérard, *L'Islande: Désert de lumière.* Reykjavik: Fjölvi, 1990

Lemarquis, Gérard, *Poésie islandaise contemporaine.* Marseille: Autres Temps, 2001

Líndal, Páll, *Reykjavik: Sögustaður við Sund 1-4.* Reykjavik: Örn og Örlygur,1989

Magnússon, Magnús Ó., *Face to face: I islandsk natur/In Icelandic Nature.* Asker, Rammetorget AS, 2001

Magnússon, Sigurður A. (trans.), *The Postwar Poetry of Iceland.* Iowa City: Iowa University Press, 1982

Morris, William, *Icelandic Journals.* Fontwell, Centaur Press, 1969

Magnusson, Magnus and Pálsson, Helmann (trans.) *Njal's Saga.* London: Penguin Books, 1960

Oslund, Karen and Cronon, William, *Iceland Imagined: Nature, Culture and Storytelling in the North Atlantic.* Seattle: University of Washington Press, 2011

Pálsson, Hermann and Magnússon, Magnús (trans.), *The Vinland Sagas: The Norse Discovery of America.* London, Penguin Books, 1965

Rosenblad, Esbjörn *et al.*, *Iceland: From Past to Present.* Reykjavik: Mál og menning, 1998

Sigurjónsdóttir, Æsa. *Islande en vue*: photographes français en Islande, 1845-1900. Reykjavik: JPV, 2000

Smiley, Jane, *The Sagas of Icelanders.* London: Penguin Books, 2005

Stefánsson, Hjörleifur, *Kvosin: Byggingarsaga miðbæjar Reykjavikur.* Reykjavik: Torfusamtökin, 1987

Thoroddsen, Jon F, *On Thin Ice.* Reykjavik: Bruduleikur, 2011

Tulinius, Torfi H, Skáldið í skriftinni: *Snorri Sturluson og Egils saga.* Reykjavik: Hið íslenska bókmenntafélag. 2004

Turville-Petre, Gabriel, *Origins of Icelandic Literature.* Oxford, Oxford University Press, 1953

Vilhjálmsson, Thor, *L'Islande*. Sommière: Romain Pages Editions, 1993

Young, Jean I. (trans.), *The Viking Gods*. 1954. Reykjavik: Guðrún, 1995

Literature

Helgason, Hallgrímur, *101 Reykjavik*. Trans. Brian FiitzGibbon. London: Faber and Faber, 2002

Indriðason, Arnaldur, *Jar City : A Reykjavik murder mystery*. Trans. Bernarnd Scudder. London: Vintage, 2009

Laxness, Halldór, *Independent People*. 1946. Trans. J. A. Thompson. New York: Vintage, 2002

Laxness, Halldór, *World Light* Trans. Magnus Magnusson. London: Everyman, 2002

Ólafsdóttir, Auður Ava, *The Greenhouse*. Trans. Brian FitzGibbon. Las Vegas: Amazon Crossing, 2009

Sigurðardóttir, Yrsa. 2010. *Ashes to Dust*. Trans. Philip Roughton. London: Hodder & Stoughton, 2011

Sjón, The Whispering Muse. Trans. Victoria Cribb. London: Telegram, 2012

Sturluson, Snorri, Edda. Trans. Anthony Faulkes. London: Everyman, 1995

Useful Websites

http://www.visitreykjavik.is/ The official tourism website of Reykjavik capital area

http://www.statice.is Hagstofa Íslands = Statistics Iceland

http://www.sedlabanki.is The Central Bank of Iceland (some information in English is to be found here)

http://www.cb.is The Central Bank of Iceland, English version

http://www.grapevine.is/Home/ The Reykjavik Grapevine is a free alternative magazine published in English

Index